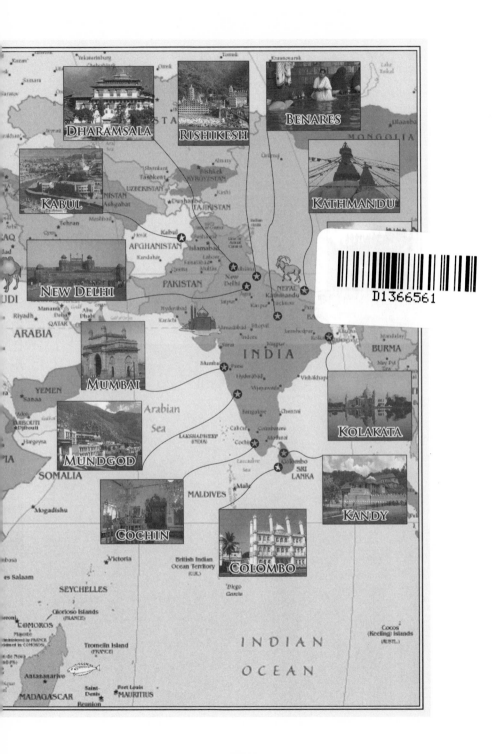

DHARAMSALA

RISHIKESH

BENARES

KABUL

KATHMANDU

NEW DELHI

MUMBAI

KOLAKATA

MUNDGOD

COCHIN

KANDY

COLOMBO

Spiritual Journey Home

Eastern Mysticism to the Western Wall

Also by Nathan Katz

Authored and Co-authored Books:

Kashrut, Caste and Kabbalah: The Religious Life of the Jews of Cochin, with Ellen
S. Goldberg (New Delhi: Manohar, 2005).

Who Are the Jews of India? (Berkeley, Los Angeles, and London: University of
California Press, 2000). **Finalist for 2000 National Jewish Book Award
(Sephardic Studies category). Winner of 2004 Vak Saraswati Sam-
man Award.**

The Last Jews of Cochin: Jewish Identity in Hindu India, with Ellen S. Goldberg.
Foreword by Daniel J. Elazar (Columbia: University of South Carolina
Press, 1993).

*Buddhist Images of Human Perfection: The Arahant of the "Sutta Pitaka" Com-
pared with the Bodhisattva and the Mahasiddha* (Delhi: Motilal Banarsidass, 1982; 2nd ed. 1989; 3rd ed. 2004).

Tampa Bay's Asian-Origin Religious Communities (Tampa: National Conference of Christians and Jews, "A Religious History of Tampa Bay," Research Reports no. 1, 1991).

Tibetan Buddhism (New Haven: Yale Divinity School, Visual Education Series,
1974).

Afghan Legends: A Textbook in Reading English as a Second Language (Kabul:
U.S. Information Service, 1972).

Edited and Co-Edited Books:

Indo-Judaic Studies in the Twenty-first Century: A View from the Margin, editor-
in-chief/co-author (with Ranabir Chakravarti, Braj M. Sinha, and Shalva
Weil), (New York: Palgrave Macmillan, 2007).

Studies of Indian-Jewish Identity, editor and co-author (New Delhi: Manohar,
1995, 2nd ed., 1999).

Ethnic Conflict in Buddhist Societies: Sri Lanka, Thailand and Burma, co-editor
and co-author with K. N. de Silva, Pensri Duke, and Ellen S. Goldberg,
(London: Frances Pinter, 1988).

Buddhist and Western Psychology, editor and co-author (Boulder, Colo.: Prajña
Press/ Shambhala, 1983).

Buddhist and Western Philosophy, editor and co-author. Foreword by H. H. the
Dalai Lama (New Delhi: Sterling, 1981).

Spiritual Journey Home

Eastern Mysticism to the Western Wall

by
Nathan Katz

KTAV Publishing House, Inc.
Jersey City, NJ

Copyright©2009 Nathan Katz

Library of Congress Cataloging-in-Publication Data

Katz, Nathan.
  Spiritual journey home : eastern mysticism to the Western Wall / Nathan
Katz.
    p. cm.
  ISBN 978-1-60280-116-5
  1. Katz, Nathan--Religion. 2. Katz, Nathan--Travel. 3. Jewish way of
life. 4. Jews--Return to Orthodox Judaism. 5. Spiritual life. 6.
Judaism--Relations--Hinduism. 7. Judaism--Relations--Buddhism. 8.
Hinduism--Relations--Judaism. 9. Buddhism--Relations--Judaism. I. Title.
  BM723.K325K37 2008
  296.7'15--dc22
                                                          2008053501

Published by
KTAV Publishing House, Inc.
930 Newark Avenue
Jersey City, NJ 07306
Email: bernie@ktav.com
www.ktav.com
(201) 963-9524
Fax (201) 963-0102

Contents

∼

Dedication

~

I lovingly dedicate this book to my son, Rafael Yechiel. Hashem gave Ellen and me this wonderful *neshamah* (soul) to nurture, and my prayer is that I have helped him to become a *mentsh*, a responsible, kindly adult who finds his own way in life, and to appreciate his life as a journey. The traditional wish Jewish parents express for their children is that they should live a life of "Torah, *chuppah*, and *ma'asim tovim*," of religious observance, finding joy in one's spouse and family, and good deeds. Amen.

Appreciation

~

I am grateful above all to my wife, Ellen, whose encouragement has been unstinting, but moreover whose support has meant assuming double duty as I left her to get the household running each morning when I went off to shul to learn and then to pray, as I traveled to India and Israel as part of the writing process, and as I spent years preoccupied with this book.

My thanks go to Florida International University for granting me a sabbatical award, and to its College of Arts and Sciences for a number of research assignments and travel grants, all of which gave me the time to reflect and to write, and to the Hindu American Foundation for a grant that enabled me to tie together loose ends just prior to publication.

During my sabbatical I was affiliated with the Centre for Advanced Historical Studies at Jawaharlal Nehru University in New Delhi and the Kogod Center for Advanced Judaic Studies at the Shalom Hartman Institute in Jerusalem. I am most grateful to these fine academic bodies for providing stimulating intellectual bases, and especially to my hosts, Professor Ranabair Chakravarti and Professor Zvi Zohar, respectively, for collegiality and friendship.

My deep thanks to Dan Wakefield, Rodger Kamenetz, Nama Frenkel, Natasha Kern, Swami Lalithananda, Sharon Hervey Rosenberg, and Ellen Goldberg for friendly support and insightful criticisms of my manuscript and to Bernie Scharfstein for his enthusiasm and professionalism. Thanks, too, to Erica Rauzin for editing and to Dara Rauzin for the fine maps. My profound respect and thanks go to my teachers, Jewish, Hindu, Buddhist, and others, many of whom are mentioned in the book.

Note

~

Of necessity, there are many Hebrew and Sanskrit terms (not to mention Aramaic, Hindi, Pali, Sinhala, Persian, Arabic, etc.) in this book. While most are defined in the text, an extensive Glossary is to be found at the end of the book. Similarly, many persons appear in my story, so we have appended a "Who's Who in This Book."

Davenen in Rishikesh: A Prologue

∾

Help me figure this out, please. Help me think this through, because this is the key to my book.

Here I am in Rishikesh, India, a medieval-like Hindu pilgrimage town on the Upper Ganges, where the Himalayan foothills begin. The streets are dusty and spackled with fresh cow dung, and the facilities are poor. Unexpectedly, I feel a sense of belonging. I have always blended in and out of multiple cultures, languages, and traditions in remote areas of the world. Even so far from home, I have often felt part of these communities. I do not understand how or why I have been blessed with this gift, or what I am to do with it.

According to Hindu sacred stories, Lord Shiva once appeared here in the form of the ascetic Rishikesh. Ever since, this little town has become a magnet for yogis, sadhus, swamis, and, yes, rishis. It is perhaps best known in the west as the place where the Beatles and Mia Farrow came to learn meditation from Maharishi Mahesh Yogi. One of the key figures of the nineteenth-century Hindu Renaissance, Swami Vivekananda, studied here. And a number of the leading religious figures of modern India—Swami Sivananda (founder of the Divine Life Society) and Chidanand Saraswati (who established Paramarth Ashram), to name two—founded spiritual communes, or ashrams, here.

I walked for miles and miles, visiting temples and ashrams, chatting with a bookstore owner, drinking tea. I encountered, amid the dust and noise and crowds, a parade with children in the garb of the gods of the Hindu pantheon, sitting regally attired on carts pulled by tractors. A stern-looking little Shiva sat cross-legged, as the Lord of the Yogis should. A young blue Krishna carried a wooden flute as a lavishly made-up little consort Radha gazed admiringly at him. Musicians in red satin pseudo-military costumes blared tubas and flugelhorns.

I loved every moment of it. Whether tranquil ashram or bustling, filthy street, I loved it. And I wonder why.

This very morning, as is my custom, I put on my prayer shawl and phylacteries, my *tallit* and *tefillin*,[1] and prayed. But here—with no classes to teach

---

[1] A *tallit* is a fringed prayer shawl, and *tefillin* are parchment Biblical verses encased in leather boxes, bound to the left arm and forehead. Observant Jewish men don *tallit* and *tefillin* for weekday morning prayers.

or meetings to attend, no mad rush to get my son to school on time—my *davenen* (praying) was more deliberate, more mindful, and more passionate than it usually is back home. There, I often have to struggle to keep up with men who have been doing this every morning since they became bar-mitzvah at age thirteen, some sixty or seventy years ago. More than that, I have to struggle to keep my focus on the prayer and its object. As often as not, I am thinking about errands to be run, papers to be written, my schedule for the day.

No, here it is different. Well, the same and different. Maybe it's that I am far from home, maybe it's that I miss my family and my comfortable routines. Maybe I need to cling all the more to my prayers, to my God. Or maybe, just maybe, there is something about being in India. Maybe India has her own reasons why I should pray deeper and harder here. In the two decades since I became religiously observant, I have noticed that *davenen* in India is different from *davenen* at home. Whether I'm alone here in the Himalayan foothills, or with a quorum for prayer in the four-centuries-old synagogue in tropical Cochin, or with a Jewish delegation to meet with the Dalai Lama in Dharamsala, I am inevitably struck that prayer becomes imbued with a richness and intensity I don't often experience back home. And I wonder why. Or maybe I don't. Without the routine, without the obligations and busy-ness of home, in India it's just me and God, one on One so to speak.

These two themes manifested in me today—my extreme sense of being at home in India, juxtaposed with my experiences of deeper levels of Jewish prayer here. These two themes, the worlds of Hinduism[2] and Judaism, are the warp and woof of my life.

------

[2] I use the word "Hinduism" much as many contemporary Hindus do, to mean the religious culture of India rather than one specific religion. It is intended to include the daughters of what we have come to call Hinduism, namely Buddhism, Jainism, and Sikhism. Historically and etymologically, the word "Hindu" is a geographic and cultural term. To the best of my knowledge, it first appears in the Talmud and was written down in the fourth century C.E.

Introduction

~

An intriguing anecdote is told about Sigmund Freud that not only crystallizes the problem of memory and narration, but also serves as a cautionary tale when writing one's memoirs. Freud was known to be as passionately curious about archaeology as he was about psychology. Jonathan Z. Smith of the University of Chicago recounts that in a 1937 letter, Freud, then eighty-one, recalled his first visit to Athens thirty-three years earlier. "When, finally . . . I stood on the Acropolis and cast my eyes around on the landscape," he wrote, "a remarkable thought suddenly entered my mind: 'So all this really *does* exist, just as we learnt at school.' "

Yet, Athens could not have existed the way Freud recalled learning about it, because the Acropolis underwent a series of major excavations between his Viennese schooldays and his 1904 visit. What we have, as Smith analyzed, "is a reminiscence . . . by an old man . . . of an experience he had in Athens at the age of forty-eight, juxtaposed to his recollection of what he learned as a teen in Vienna's Sperlgymnasium."

Philosophers have argued that all instances of memory are fraught with similar difficulties. In remembering, we filter, edit, and select from among past experiences. Quite literally, we re-member, creating something new in the act of remembering, thus producing our own myth about ourselves.

In other words, while a book of memoirs seems to be about the past, it uses bits and pieces from the past to construct a narrative in the present. This memoir is, then, more about who I am *now* than who I was *then*. It is not that I haven't tried my level best to be accurate, but accuracy is not exactly the same as honesty. Constructing this narrative has been humbling, because I have become aware of how active a role my inner narrator has played in putting this story together.

My inner narration keeps bringing me back to my dining room. Soon after moving to Miami, when my wife and I were house hunting, the spacious dining room was what most attracted me to the then-run-down house where we've subsequently lived for a decade and a half. My mind's eye saw a dozen guests sitting around an oak table adorned with white linen, our best china, good wine, and bright flowers. My inner ear heard spirited debates about mystical interpretations of the Torah, interspersed with boisterous Hebrew songs with melodies from India and Yemen. I heard children and adults laughing together, and I felt my hand reach to touch my wife's so gently.

I saw a fulfilled life in a redeemed world.

Torah teaches us that ever since the destruction of the Temple of Jerusalem, the dining table (*shulhan*) in our home has fulfilled the sacred role of the Altar in the Temple (*shulhan ha-mizbe'ah*). Both tables are bridges between us and God. In ancient times we used the priestly-sacrificial system that the Romans ended in the year 70 of the common era. Our rabbis, with spiritual genius, pointed us to our own homes, our own mundane lives, to replicate what before was only done through elaborate rites in one of the most spectacular edifices of the ancient world.

In other words, the deepest spiritual truths are right here in front of us, hiding behind their appearance as the mundane. Our task as humans is how to see what is right there in front of us, and to live consciously in the continuous presence of the sacred. While it took me an extended excursus to Hindu ashrams, Sufi brotherhoods, and Buddhist meditation centers to capture that appreciative vision, in order to live my daily life in the presence of the sacred I found my path, predictably, right in my own family, traditions, and background. In its insistence on detail, Orthodox Judaism shows me again and again to "Know before Whom you stand,"[1] how to eat at this sacred table.

Coming from a lukewarm, traditional Jewish background, it took a remarkable visionary encounter in late-1960s Kathmandu to direct my steps on a path that led me to my dining table.

Awaiting sleep in my small bedroom in a rambling house near Bouddhanath, a Buddhist pilgrimage point outside of Kathmandu, I felt the presence of an intruder. Turning toward it, I was alarmed that an old beggar woman was beside me, palms extended accompanied by a plaintive wail of "*Paisa, paisa*" ("Coins, coins"). Like many first-time visitors to the subcontinent, the beggars had appalled me, and this one, though slight of frame, seemed especially ominous. Fear and anger rose in mind, and I raised my arm to brush away her extended hand—but my hand passed right through her! I turned my back, my mind and my heart racing as my body stiffened and my nerves screamed. From

---

[1] The singular form of the charge in *Berakhot* 28b, prominently displayed in many synagogues. Cf. *Pirkei Avot* 2:19.

somewhere, I heard wisdom: "If you feel love for her, she will stop bothering you." So I turned, still fearful but somehow generating affection for her. The swiftest of faint smiles crossed her lips and she was gone.

At first I thought she was a ghost. To this day I am not sure whether she was a hallucination or a dream or a goddess or the Holy Shekhinah (Divine Presence) Herself. In any case, her presence was simultaneously repulsive and attractive. Mystical literature, whether the Hebrew Book of Job or the Sanskrit *Bhagavad Gita*, describes the Divine-human encounter as "awe-ful," that when standing before the Divine we are powerfully attracted and just as powerfully frightened and repelled. So we "tremble" or "quake" before the whirlwind that is how God appears to Job, or before Krishna's fearsome "true form" (*swarupanarayanan*) that shatters Arjuna's sense of sanity. Soon after I met this frightening, ugly, yet profoundly attractive presence, I understood that my life would forever be different, that my path had unexpected twists in store for me.

First through the archetypical psychology of Carl Jung, and then decades of study of mysticisms and literatures, especially Buddhist, slowly I came to understand that my intellect was not my core, that my mind is more than my brain, and that my heart is as sure a source of wisdom as my reason. This crone, whatever she was, taught me all this and much more over the years. I learned later that in medieval Buddhist literature she is called a *dakini*, literally a "sky-goer." Jung called her the *anima*, or soul, a symbolic and highly potent manifestation of the unconscious.

Understood this way, I have come to believe that I glimpsed her again, years later, in the holy city of Tsfat (Safed in English) in the mountains of northern Israel, the greatest center of the study of Kabbalah. In the Hasidic Bratslaver synagogue, worshippers welcomed Shabbat with song and dance, circling the large sanctuary with spiraling intensity, clapping and jumping. As the frenzy peaked, I glanced toward the women's section upstairs hoping for a glimpse of my wife. And there the Sabbath Queen was, a fleeting presence for sure, but right there standing beside my wife!

Over the years, as I got to know her better, she transformed from a frightening hag into my family's most honored guest at our table, the Sabbath Queen. She has become as familiar as she was once unexpected; She brings blessings of contentment and occasionally bestows glimpses of her divinity. She reveals the sacredness of my table. In no small measure, the story I have to tell is about this process of transformation that is reflected in my apperceptions of her, and her interdependence with actual women, foremost my wife, who similarly can inspire adoration and occasionally fear.

And as is so for everyone, my story is about loss and gain. Especially powerful were our struggles with infertility and a miscarriage. Having chosen to follow a spiritual path in which children are essential, one that is so thoroughly rooted in the family and situated around our sacred table in the home, it seemed that our inability to produce offspring closed off our access to aspirations, both mundane and spiritual. My story, like everyone's story, is about understanding loss as redirection, a gift, and that as soon as one door closes, another opens, if we can be patient enough to new possibilities. This is known in Judaism as *bitahon*, trust in the L-rd, an ever-present readiness to find spiritual opportunity at every turn in the road.

Newly observant Jews have written intriguing books about their journeys of *teshuvah* (literally, "return" to a traditional practice of Judaism). Most of the authors now reject their past experiments with yoga or *vipassana* meditation, and I guess that is where we differ. One of my teachers, Chögyam Trungpa, used to teach that "the journey is the goal," and I embrace where I am and how I got here. I also add the proviso that this book does not attempt to speak for anyone other than myself, least of all does it claim to represent Orthodox Judaism. Jewish law defines two categories of permissible actions. Some acts are permissible beforehand, *le-kha-tehillah*. Others are permissible only after the fact, *be-di-avad*. So I wonder. Surely my meanderings from the synagogue to the ashram to the monastery and back to the synagogue would not be permissible *le-kha-tehillah*. But perhaps *be-di-avad*? While I would not recommend that anyone else should follow my path, perhaps, nevertheless, it can be seen positively in retrospect, from the perspective of Orthodox Judaism.

My personal spiritual journey interweaves Israel and India. So does my professional life, and I am grateful for and proud of this unexpected convergence of inner and outer. I was trained in Indology, the study of classical India, but happenstance led my wife and me to a year living with the ancient Jewish community in Cochin, South India. As my spiritual eye shifted from swamis and lamas to rabbis, so my professional life moved from Sanskrit and Tibetan texts to the interactions and affinities between Indic and Judaic civilizations, a field of study I call "Indo-Judaic Studies." What began as an eccentric wrinkle in my study of India became the professional focus of my career.

I celebrate my personal and professional links between India and Israel. I have been ahead of the curve in this, and it is with a deep sense of gratification that I see others moving in that direction. In particular, the meeting in New Delhi in February 2007, between the Chief Rabbi of Israel and the Head of the Hindu Dharma Acharya Sabha, confirmed much of what I have believed for decades. At this watershed event, the rabbis and swamis affirmed that they worship the same God and that this God intentionally created the world to be religiously diverse.[2] For once, but probably not once and for all, the Judaic issue of "idolatry," or *avodah zarah*, has been swept off the dialogical table.

I don't claim to have the answers, but my hope is simply to tell the story of my own unexpected journey, the discovery of my sacred table.

---

[2] See Meylekh Vishwanath, "The Hindu-Jewish Encounter, New Delhi, February 2007," *Journal of Indo-Judaic Studies* 9 (2007): 102–111.

THE SACRED TABLE

~

It is written: The Altar (*mizbe'ah*) was of wood, three *ammot* [= 4.5 feet] high, and its length two *ammot*, and its corners and its length and walls of wood. And he [i.e., the angel] said to me: "This is the Table (*shulhan*) that is before Hashem [God].". . .

[The *Gemara* (later sections of the Talmud) analyzes it:] [The verse] began with "the Altar" but ended with "the Table." [Why does it call the Table "the Altar"?]

[The *Gemara* explains:] Rabbi Yohanan and Reish Lakish both said: [It is to teach the following lesson.] During the period in which the Holy Temple stood, the Altar would atone for a person. Now [that the Temple is destroyed], a person's table atones for him.

Babylonian Talmud, *Hagigah* 27a

1

The Light of Childhood
Camden, New Jersey

⌇

When I think about my spiritual meanderings from shul to ashram and back, my thoughts turn to my childhood in the 1950s in Camden, New Jersey. Perhaps more than I'd care to admit, my spiritual tastes and interests have their roots in our neighborhood and synagogues there.

Camden. The very name is synonymous with urban decay and violence. The national news recently profiled it as "the most dangerous city in America." I do not doubt that it is. Not long ago, I took my then thirteen-year-old son there to show him where I grew up. I think he was rather horrified—especially compared with our posh Miami Beach life. The house where I grew up is, of course, much smaller than I remembered. But my parents, two older brothers, and I lived there quite happily, even though it is probably less than half the size of the house where my wife, son, and I live today. One car, one bathroom, and one television—that was middle-class American family life in the 1950s, and none of us felt in the least deprived. We had all we needed and most of what we wanted.

In those days, Camden was a thriving industrial city of 125,000. It was home to Walt Whitman, Campbell Soup, RCA, New York Shipyards, Parker Pens, Whitman's Chocolates, good hotels, shopping, and entertainment. Today, all of the industries have moved away. The population has shrunk to 80,000, mostly underclass African Americans and Latinos. Remembering what she once was, all of Camden's former residents are saddened by her humbled state. Camden today is a town without even a movie theater or supermarket, and the only occupied buildings in its forlorn downtown are government offices, courthouses, and a pleasant little branch campus of Rutgers University, where my eldest brother Sid taught chemistry until he retired last year.

My family was traditional. We usually prayed at Beth El, the large Conservative synagogue a block from our home on Park Boulevard, then a fashionable street in a neighborhood called Parkside, but now filled with

3

boarded-up crack houses. As a youngster, I was a regular most Shabbat mornings at the synagogue's junior congregation downstairs, although some of the time I remember sitting beside my parents upstairs in the main sanctuary.

A Career as a Rabbi?

I was enamored of the rabbi, a handsome and eloquent man. For some years, I wanted to follow him into the rabbinate. I enjoyed praying and even led the services in the junior congregation. I may have been the only boy my age who knew the liturgy well enough to lead the services, but my utter inability to carry a tune embarrassed me. Vainly, I implored my friends to lead at least some of the chants, but they either did not know how or simply did not care to try. So there I was, croaking away on the *bimah* (dais), alternatively experiencing the joy of prayer and the agony of each misplaced note.

When I was upstairs in the main sanctuary, especially during the High Holy Days, the *Aron ha-Kodesh* (the Holy Ark where Torah scrolls are kept) fascinated me. I fancied that I saw light emerging from behind the Ark's wooden doors. I even felt moments in the beautiful sanctuary when the choir and the open Ark seemed to produce a blaze of light and an elevated feeling. "Holy! Holy! Holy is the L-rd of Hosts (*Kadosh! Kadosh! Kadosh, Ad-nai Tziva'ot*)," the choir sang, and I felt their words and tunes penetrate me to the core. These experiences became a focal point of my religious life. As I matured, I continually sought to recreate them.

My maternal grandparents, Henry and Tillie Gelb, who lived behind a storefront on the commercial street a few blocks away, were Orthodox. My grandfather had a special influence on me. Sometimes I met him at the Congregation Sons of Israel, the Orthodox shul that was two blocks beyond the Conservative synagogue on Park Boulevard.[1] I have fond memories of playing under my grandfather's *tallit* (prayer shawl), and of feeling a sense of mystery as I strained for a peek at my grandmother, who prayed behind the *mehitzah* (barrier between the men's and women's sections in an Orthodox synagogue). I also remember an occasional family *simhah* (life-cycle ritual celebration) at B'nai Avrohom, a small shul in a more modest part of town on Liberty Street, just a few doors from an uncle's junkyard. If memory serves me, that little shul looked rather like the *shtibl* (small storefront synagogue) where I *davn* and learn now in Miami Beach.

---

[1] *Shul*, Yiddish for "school," is how Orthodox Jews most often refer to their house of worship. While there is no hard-and-fast rule, Conservative Jews generally call it a synagogue, and Reform Jews, a temple.

In those days, there wasn't so much difference between Orthodox and Conservative Judaism. Everyone "kept kosher" (observed the dietary laws) after a fashion, and no one drove on Shabbat. The chief differences were that in Conservative synagogues, families sat together, and the rabbi was clean-shaven and spoke in English. While I admired the Conservative rabbi's eloquence, I was struck by the passion of the Orthodox rabbi's talks in Yiddish, even though I understood only a little.

I admired both rabbis. The Conservative one must remain anonymous, and the Orthodox one was the reputed scholar Naphtali Riff. Adults who asked were bemused when I said I wanted to be a rabbi when I grew up. I never did fulfill this ambition, not yet anyway, and one of the reasons for my youthful disillusionment with the profession was that the Conservative rabbi, whom I sought to emulate, became involved in a scandal and was forced from his pulpit. Like many clergy, he indulged in a peccadillo with a congregant. This bothered me. In my young mind, rabbis simply didn't do that sort of thing; I thought that holy people would not take sexual liberties. But, as Freud taught us about the psychological mechanism of transference, anyone in a position of authority—from psychotherapist to Catholic priest to guru to professor—can and, alas, all too often does, exercise power. Later in my life I experienced any number of similar disappointments with lamas, swamis, and masters. While I am no longer so surprised by these shenanigans, I am still disappointed and disillusioned. I wonder whether these clergy know how deeply their failings affect their congregants, who tend to idealize them. Their personal frailties can damage the very faith of those whom they try to serve.

Both of my neighborhood synagogues felt cozy, or *heymish* ("homey"), as we'd say in Yiddish. I especially loved standing in front of the Conservative synagogue after Shabbat services, exchanging greetings both with our fellow congregants and those from the Orthodox shul who strolled by. Everyone knew everybody else; I was known in the context of my parents, grandparents, uncles, aunts, and cousins, and I felt a deep sense of security in this familial circle.

My parents, Charles and Frances Katz, worked hard in their small neon sign business. They charged five dollars to "remove, repair, and reinstall" a Camden Beer sign anywhere in South Jersey. They had a shop on the commercial street with an apartment above for my brother when he first married, a Chevrolet pickup truck, and a part-time glassblower. At home, we had an extension of the shop telephone, and in the kitchen, a filing cabinet and a typewriter for doing the billing on Sunday mornings.

Born in the village of Dinowitz, Ukrainia, in 1909, my father was named for his uncle, Yechiel, and in turn my son is named for him. Only recently did I learn Uncle Yechiel's story. He was a soldier in Siberia in the czar's army during the Russo-Japanese War. As Passover was approaching, he and some other Jewish conscripts decided to bake *matzah* indoors, and the smoke from the fire asphyxiated them and they all died. In the Jewish world, to die while fulfilling a *mitzvah*, a commandment, is a *Kiddush Hashem*, a "sanctification of God's name," and my son is proud of his ancestor. My father could be jovial, which is how my cousins remember him, but he also had a brutal temper. He found humor in devising a "cat o' nine tails" to whip me into shape, but I also felt his love, his pride in me, and his disappointments with me.

My mother's family came from Budapest, a cosmopolitan contrast to Dinowitz. Her father, both knowledgeable and pious, was a student of Rabbi Riff, and I enjoyed visiting him after school and trying to solve his Talmud-based riddles. I remember shoveling coal from the bin into his furnace, and even seeing carp in the bathtub for the gefilte fish, a special treat for the Shabbat table.

I was named for my father's father, Naftali. As is Ashkenazi (East European) custom, a child is named only for deceased ancestors, and tradition says that something of the deceased is reincarnated into the namesake. My eldest first cousin, now in her mid-eighties, tells me that my grandfather was an excellent cook, which was unusual for a Jewish man a century ago; it is also striking, because cooking is one of my pleasures.

My father got through the ninth grade, always struggling with English. My mother was a high school graduate, which was pretty high-falutin' in my father's mind—and also a bit intimidating for him. Not educated himself, he made sure that his children would be well schooled, and all three of us became college professors.

My eldest brother, Sid, thirteen years my senior, was something of a rebel: James Dean–style hair, a yellow Ford convertible, and a well-muscled body. But before he became so cool, I remember him spending time in an iron lung because of a bout with polio during his mid-teens. When he was ill, I remember hearing my father sobbing in fear, which frightened me. When Sid recovered, he became the favorite and later he turned "wild," getting into various sorts of trouble. He got a job at the Hollingshead Chemical Company after graduating from high school and from that moment on, his life found a course, culminating in a doctorate from the University of Pennsylvania and a long, distinguished career teaching chemistry at Rutgers University.

My other brother, Ellis, was milder, and since we were a bit closer in age, I felt closer to him. He was the one who took me to Phillies games, where I enjoyed the brilliantly green playing field at Connie Mack Stadium where Robin Roberts and Richie Ashburn led our boys to year after year of futility. Ellis was a college man as I approached puberty, and I thought his Rutgers fraternity house was the coolest place to be. The ethos of an early 1960s campus shaped me—chinos and loafers, vocal jazz, and *Playboy* magazine, defined all that hipness meant. After Rutgers, Ellis went to Columbia for his doctorate in political science and became a professor at Temple University, where he spent his career.

Two brothers, two professors, two jobs, each with one wife and two kids. I had a lot to live up to, so it seemed to me.

Community, Community, Community

Parkside was a cozy neighborhood. My uncle was the kosher butcher, and on the same commercial street as his shop was a kosher bakery run by my mother's uncle, another uncle's appliance repair business, and my father's neon sign shop. A couple of blocks beyond was another uncle's propane gas business and yet another uncle's washing machine repair service. The neighborhood had a movie theater, toy store, men's shop, paint store, and so on. We knew all the neighborhood merchants by name, and they knew ours, because we all lived in the same neighborhood. So did the postman, the florist, and my schoolteachers. It was the kind of world where I was enthralled when my teacher would walk home with me for lunch. It was also a self-contained world. After school, I would visit my grandparents, or an aunt, or some of my school pals. My world felt safe with so many familiar adults and friends around.

I spent the first half of my adult life in an attempt to recover both the spirituality of my childhood shul and the closeness of my neighborhood. I eventually managed to do so, but that is the end of my story, and we're just getting started.

When our family moved to Parkside, the neighborhood was mostly Jewish, but there were also some African Americans and a few Italians. We felt entirely comfortable with them all, and my mother's active role in the PTA ensured that our social network extended beyond just family and synagogue.

Then came the 1960s and the breakdown of that sense of community. My personal teenage rebellion coincided with a culture of rebelliousness, just at the moment when the restraints of a traditional community unraveled. As African Americans moved in greater numbers into Parkside, Jews began moving to the suburbs in the infamous "white flight." My family, comfortable in our changing neighborhood and with no special animus toward blacks, resisted the change.

Conservative synagogues anticipated the demographic shift, and in 1950 the Conservative movement issued a landmark legal ruling permitting its members to drive to and from synagogue on Shabbat and holy days. Better to remove the prohibition against driving and have people attend synagogue, it was reasoned, than to hold fast to *Halakhah* (Judaic law) and risk having near-empty synagogues. Those Jews who spread out to the suburbs, miles from synagogues, received rabbinical approval to drive and pray rather than stay home and not pray. And while the synagogues may have remained reasonably full, traditional Jewish neighborhoods broke down.

Now there were no neighbors to scold rowdy children, or to keep a watchful eye on them. Now it was no longer possible to stroll to a bustling, familiar commercial street; instead, we drove to a shopping center where the shopkeepers were anonymous, and so were we. This was the dawning of the age of alienation, a precursor to Aquarius.

A Hindu in the Woods

Right before I was born, my parents bought a summer cabin on the Rancocas Creek in Mount Holly, New Jersey. It was a modest place. We had to boil water on the propane stove (thanks, Uncle Dave) for our infrequent baths, and for the first several years we had only an outhouse for our bodily needs. Years later when I showed it to my dissertation adviser—a brilliant, eccentric scholar named Bibhuti S. Yadav who hailed from a village in the general area of Benares—he dubbed it "the hut," and since the name was apt, it stuck. The woodsy atmosphere offered a respite from the summer heat in Camden, and I spent huge parts of my summer days swimming and canoeing in the creek. Every Sunday, hordes of city-dwelling relatives and friends would arrive, and my father would fire up a charcoal grill for the meat and boil water in a huge kettle for the sweet Jersey corn.

A hermit artist by the name of Hugh Campbell lived not far along the dirt trail. He became a sort of pied piper for the many children whose families had nearby summer cottages. We especially loved his duck calls, and were utterly befuddled by his vegetarianism. He was one of the few adults who seemed to have the time to really talk with us, and he told stories about the yogis and mystics of India.

Years later he self-published a book of autobiographical poems, and I then learned that he had become an initiate in the Ramakrishna Order, a prominent non-dualist, modern Hindu movement, and had studied with a number of great teachers. I guess that what all our religions teach us is true: that there are no accidents in life, that Divine Providence reigns in our day-to-day lives, or that whatever we experience is a result of our past actions or karma. How else can I make sense of the curious fact that when I was only eight or ten, one of our neighbors in the woods of New Jersey was a Hindu adept?

Jazz

Saturdays were Shabbatot, of course, spent for the most part with family and friends. But Sundays were also special, because as I entered my teen years I would generally hang out with my black friends after they returned home from church. We would wander from house to house, eating exotic-tasting food, and exchanging news and gossip while jazz played on the FM radio.

In this environment I came to love jazz, even as a youth. As I grew into my middle teen years, my friends and I began to haunt the jazz clubs of downtown Philly or, in the summertime, in Atlantic City. We'd catch Ray Charles at the Latin Casino nightclub in suburban Cherry Hill or in West Philadelphia's concert halls—these moments were the richest spiritual experiences of my teen years.

I also loved writing. By high school, I was editor of both the school newspaper and the literary magazine. I wrote poems, stories, essays, anything. So it was not long before I combined my two passions, writing and jazz. I was precocious as well as audacious (*chutspadik*, as we say), so by the age of fourteen, I was requesting—and getting—interviews with the jazz greats who came to town. I interviewed Cannonball Adderley, Yusuf Lateef, Gloria Lynn, and Maynard Ferguson. And I went so far as to submit one of my interviews to *Jazz Magazine*, then second only to *Down Beat* in the field, and it even got accepted for publication. I recall it so well: the editor asked for a biographical note on me, and I sent one back mentioning that I was fourteen. I guess he was embarrassed to have accepted a piece by a kid, and I never heard from him again. My disappointment and sense of injustice depressed me for fully a year, and I learned that it is not always wise to be quite so forthcoming.

Jazz went deep; it touched me in a way that I sensed as similar to my experiences with the light of the synagogue Ark. More than any other event in my teens, I reached my spiritual pinnacle hearing John Coltrane play at the Showboat Lounge on South Street in Philadelphia. Even though I had no musical talent whatsoever, I felt as if I could see each note and somehow understand that Coltrane's wailing scales were stairways to heaven, as the old ballad goes. His music still transports me. I also heard Ravi Shankar at Philadelphia's gorgeous Academy of Music. Years later, as I became more and more enamored of India, I found much the same spirituality in Indian classical *ragas* and *bhajans*. The structures of jazz and classical Indian music strike me as being so similar: a basic tune, dazzling rhythms, spontaneous improvisations, and especially the remarkable nonverbal communication among the performers and with the audience. With both of these forms of music, I feel that one actually participates in the creativity simply by listening intently.

My family stayed in Camden until I graduated from high school. When I went off to college, my parents sold the house and bought a condo—a one-bedroom apartment at that! I was on my own: new friends, new intellectual vistas, and no neighbors' watchful eyes. While I embraced my freedom and all the trouble I could find, I was already becoming nostalgic for what was no more. Instead of a hearty greeting of "*Gut Shabbos*" to neighbors clad in fedoras and stoles, now I conjured ersatz-community by flashing peace signs to fellow longhairs in paisley shirts and love beads. I sought to recapture that light blazing from the *Aron ha-Kodesh* with mescaline and LSD.

A Childhood Prophecy

My mother (may her memory be a blessing) used to tell this story: When I was five years old, I solemnly announced to the family at the Friday night Shabbos table that I intended to go to India at my first opportunity. I don't recall what prompted this outbreak of *nevu'ah* (prophecy), whether it was something I had read or a travelogue I had seen, but I lived up to it.

Naturally enough, I am often asked to explain my passion for India. The truth of the matter is, I am as befuddled by it as the person asking the question, likely more so. For as long as I can remember, India has been part of me. When I was a pre-teen, like most boys at the time, I collected postage stamps. I occasionally took the bus to the Lit Brothers department store in Philadelphia's Center City to spend my one-dollar weekly allowance at the stamp department. I attended weekly stamp club meetings at the suburban Jewish community center, where I discovered that most of my pals collected American or Israeli stamps, while I treasured the ones from India or Burma or Laos.

I cannot explain it at all, but, of course, my Indian friends can. With knowing smiles, they tell me that in my last life I was most assuredly Indian. And since I have come to learn that reincarnation (*gilgul* in Hebrew) is a basic assumption in Judaism's esoteric traditions, who I am to deny it?

2

Meeting the *Dakini*
Kathmandu

~

True to the vow I made at the tender age of five, when my first opportunity to go to India presented itself, I seized upon it eagerly. In 1969, when I was twenty, some friends from my hippie crowd in Philadelphia were holed up somewhere in Nepal and invited me to come. They had a big house with plenty of room, and living there was so cheap that pretty much all I would need was a plane ticket. In those days, a round trip cost the princely sum of $450, but I was able to scare up the money, and as soon as the spring semester ended, I was off.

I am still not sure why I did it, and I cannot say my motives were entirely noble. Perhaps a simple sense of adventure, something I retain to this day, was the main impetus. Another factor was spiritual longing. I had dabbled with yoga, meditation, and the like, and I reasoned that such things were on every street corner in that part of the world. A less savory motivation was that hashish was said to be legal, cheap, plentiful, and powerful over there. And finally, in the sixties, it was a cool thing to do. If the Beatles went to Rishikesh, shouldn't I follow their lead to the Himalayas?

Dizzying Delhi

Nothing possibly could have prepared me for the overstimulation of the senses that greets every first-time traveler to India. As is still the case, international flights arrive in the middle of the night. I can still hear the words of the flight attendant as we alighted: "Welcome to New Delhi. The local time is 3:30 a.m., and the local temperature is 96 degrees." I was sure she had make a mistake—until the sultry, pungent air hit me with a blast as I clambered down the stairway. After getting colorful visa stamps in my fresh passport and retrieving my backpack from Customs, I found a yellow-and-black Ambassador taxi. It looked like something from a 1930s gangster movie, but in India it was the latest model. I was exhausted by the flight, which in those days made many stops and took much longer than today's still grueling twenty-plus hours.

I had no idea of where to go, so the taxi driver deposited me at a "very fine" hotel located on Connaught Circus, the city's colorful hub. As it was the middle of the night, I saw nothing of the world outside. The bearer took me to a large room with twenty-foot ceilings, very little furniture, and a whirring ceiling fan suspended at the end of a ten-foot pole. It was the first time I had ever seen a ceiling fan, and I was terrified that when I stood up it would cut off my head, even though it was still ten feet above the floor. The bathroom with its stark shower, bare concrete floor, and eastern-style toilet appalled me. I could not sleep, and after a couple of hours the now-familiar Indian morning sounds pierced the darkness. As soon as it was light, I ventured outside.

Even that early, the town was buzzing. Scooters, taxis, diesel-belching buses, hand carts pulled by scrawny turbaned men, tea sellers, horrifying-looking beggars, and hawkers of every imaginable variety—and some not even imaginable!—were everywhere. India, especially in those days, was just so utterly different from anything in my frame of reference that I immediately began to doubt the wisdom of my decision to come.

That doubt was quickly reinforced. I crossed the road into the park-like center of the roundabout, and immediately a shoeshine boy offered his services. I told him my shoes were not dirty, and he immediately threw whitewash on them. "Yes, sahib. Very dirty. Shoes shined? One rupee only." I responded as any proud Camden boy might, knocking him to the ground before me and demanding that he clean them, which he did with furtive glances at this overly aggressive foreigner.

The next moment, a woman with a child came up to me with a smiling, "*Namaste*," and pinned a paper poppy flower to my shirt. "Children's day, sahib. You take flower. Ten rupees (then about $1.25) please." I gave her one rupee, and to her curses—I imagined that is what she was shrieking as a crowd gathered around us—turned and retreated to my hotel for refuge from the bewildering Indian street.

I wrote a postcard to a college buddy. I wish I still had it, but I recall writing that this was worse than the worst of the Lower East Side, which in those pre-gentrification days was pretty bad.

Even though it was morning by the clock, to me it was evening and I was hungry. I went into the hotel restaurant, which was lined with musty, heavy velvet curtains. Once upon a time, this had been an elegant British hotel, but it surely didn't strike me that way. The waiter was a stately Sikh with a huge red turban, starched white trousers, and gold braids adorning his flowing Nehru coat. And this was at breakfast! He looked so distinguished and I felt so grubby that I wanted to seat him at my table and run to the kitchen to fetch him a coffee. Here I was, a twenty-year-old hippie, filled with American egalitarian assumptions. How could I accept food service from someone who looked so much more distinguished and imposing than I?

Since I was in India, I wanted to try curry, and being a gracious host, the Sikh offered to get me chicken curry with rice and dal, even though it was breakfast time. After just a couple of bites, I panicked. It tasted so incredibly hot to my American palate. I wondered how I was ever going to eat anything in this place. I called for water and drank it by the quart. That was my first mistake. For one thing, water does not mitigate the heat of chilies; that is why Indians serve yogurt side dishes. Drinking water to soothe an overly heated mouth is like pouring gasoline to douse flames. For another thing, back in those days one simply didn't drink the tap water in Delhi, especially if one's stomach was unaccustomed to it. So I spent the rest of the day in my room, drinking thermos after thermos of water to no avail, and visiting the odd-looking toilet more times than I can remember.

With such an introduction, it is little wonder that I was tempted to head right back to the airport and the relative serenity of Philadelphia. But I didn't, and the next day I had an experience that has stayed with me ever since.

I was walking past the Imperial Hotel near Connaught. As its name implies, it had been a bastion of British India, though by 1969 it was somewhat run down. Since then it has been renovated, and it is now my family's favorite, even if we can't really afford it.

As I was walking, a Sikh approached me. "Excuse me, sir. I will bet you ten rupees that I can tell you your favorite flower, your birth date, and your mother's first name." It seemed like a sure thing to me, but like most sure things, it wasn't. I deliberately tried to make my mind blank as he stared intently at me. He said a rose, which I figured played with the odds. Then he correctly told me my birth date, and I reasoned that since I had provided that information to the desk clerk when I checked into my hotel, the two might be in cahoots. Then he told me my mother's first and maiden names, and I couldn't rationalize that. Next he offered to tell my future, but I declined. "Why not, sir? Have I not correctly revealed your favorite flower, your birth date, and your mother's name?" I told him that indeed he had, and that was precisely why I did not want him to tell me my future. He just might have been able to discern that too.

Later I asked Indian friends about this trick, and I was assured it was very genuine, but no big deal. "Oh, yes," I was told. "These Sardarjis (how Sikhs are respectfully called in India) have a special place where they learn how to pluck this from our minds. But that is all they can do, no more."

About four years later, my mother was to visit me in India. We stayed at the Imperial, since she was footing the bill, and it was no surprise to me that the same Sikh approached her and provided the same information. To her dying day, she was certain I had set it up. Recently, when I was leading a high-end tour of North India, we again stayed at the Imperial, and one of the guests on my tour had the same experience, but this time with the grandson of the original mind reader. He hasn't gotten over it, either.

Kathmandu

After a while in India, I flew up to Kathmandu. I ended up spending my twenty-first birthday there, which somehow seemed appropriate. My hippie friends from Philadelphia met me at Tribhuvan Airport. They stuffed my backpack into the trunk of the taxi, and we sped off. Soon, we were walking around the oldest part of town. Even seasoned as I was by four or five days in Delhi, Kathmandu was something else again. It was positively medieval, with narrow streets, open sewers, and more pagoda-style temples than I could count. Oddly, the more exotic the place appeared, the more I felt at home.

I loved Kathmandu at once. Unabashedly, people stopped in the street to pray at tiny shrines or to relieve themselves, with equal abandon. Their smiles were forthcoming and genuine. The town had virtually no tourist facilities except for two five-star hotels, which refused to serve even take-out sandwiches to hippies like us. The other end of the spectrum was Freak Street, the hippie enclave with cheap, dirty restaurants serving some vague semblance of European food, cruddy hotels, and hashish cafes with hi-fi sets blasting the Beatles and the Rolling Stones. When I was in Kathmandu most recently in 2002, I was surprised to see that the anonymous alley bore official street signs marking it as "Freak Street," a sort of commemoration of the 1960s.

My friends had rented a large two-story house near a serene place called Bouddhanath, which was then surrounded by rice paddies. The house had practically no furnishings, the electricity failed several times a day, and the toilets flushed directly outside, where pigs slurped the refuse. Today development has caught up with the place. Not only does Bouddhanath have tourist hotels and several Dharma centers catering to foreign seekers, but also Kathmandu has grown so extensively that Bouddhanath is now just another neighborhood amid the urban sprawl. Bouddhanath is renown for its imposing *stupa*, a 117-foot-tall Buddhist reliquary with four pairs of painted Dharma eyes, one facing each compass point, symbolic of the omniscience of enlightenment. It was not until some years after my first visit that I learned that Bouddhanath is also one of the most sacred places in all of Mahayana Buddhism, said to have been constructed by Guru Rinpoche, the eighth-century Indian Tantric saint credited with introducing Buddhism into Tibet. But at the time I simply found the place strange.

The godfather of the town was a lama who ruled the sacred complex. He was said to have eight wives. The lama was our landlord and a wheeler-dealer of the first order. I purchased a lovely Tibetan carpet from him for $60. I still have it. He traded in opium and women too, I was told. I also learned that in addition to profiteering for himself, he used his ill-gotten money to support any number of monks and nuns who had fled to Nepal from Chinese-occupied Tibet.

So the days passed in Nepal. We frequently walked around the nooks and crannies of Kathmandu and the other cities in the valley, Patan and Bhaktipur. The latter, especially, charmed me, with its brick buildings and ornately carved wooden window frames. It boasts some of the finest, most graceful temples in all Nepal, and is now a world heritage site. This means not only that it is being preserved, but also that foreigners must pay in dollars just to stroll its lanes and squares. We made an expedition to Pokhara, a gorgeous village with an unparalleled view of massive Annapurna, and we trekked for several days along the fabled Jomson Trail, among the most beautiful spots on the planet.

Meeting the *Dakini*

Like most visitors to this part of the world, I found the beggars unnerving. Wretched-looking creatures, these poor souls accost everyone, especially foreigners, beseeching them for a few rupees for food. Some were hideously deformed; others simply dirty and disheveled. I learned to give them charity furtively, lest their colleagues overwhelm me with their demands. Their cries of "*Paisa, paisa*" ("Coins, coins") are haunting—especially the pleas of women with naked babies at their withered breasts.

One evening as I was lying down waiting for sleep, I was startled by a sensed presence in my little bedroom. I turned and to my horror found an especially frightening-looking old woman in the room with me, her hands silently gesturing her demand for coins. I told her to go away and leave me alone, but she drew closer, continuing to gesture for coins. In frustration, I reached out to knock her hand away. . . . But my hand passed right through her arm! I jumped against the bedside wall and turned my back, my heart pounding, and my mind racing. A ghost! I had never seen one, but this must be such an apparition. Somewhere from within my mind a thought reached my consciousness: Open your heart to her and she will leave you alone. I gulped down my fear and turned to face her. Wanly, I smiled a faint smile and felt a glimmer of love, and she vanished. I rolled over, burying my head in my arms and slowly rocking myself to sleep.

That presence was with me the moment I awoke. What was this? Was I going mad? Did other people see such things? I kept these thoughts to myself for several days before asking my friends whether the house was haunted. Predictably, they rolled their eyes. "Are you getting weird on us?" was all they said. I was alone with my vision.

I tried and tried to dismiss what I had experienced, but I couldn't. Was it a dream? Was I mad? It didn't feel like either. This was so real; it was like no dream I had ever had, and I felt no madder than before. I became compelled, driven, to understand this event, so utterly unlike anything I had known.

I decided it was getting to be time for me to go home.

When I got back to Philadelphia, I began to read. Somehow, somewhere, there was an explanation. Someone must know what this was all about. But who? Intuitively, I began to read Carl Jung. After some time I stumbled across his concept of the *anima,* and I felt I was reading about what I had experienced. I asked and searched and probed, and eventually learned that there was a psychiatrist in Philadelphia who had actually studied with Jung, a Quaker gentleman named Robert A. Clark. During our first session I told him my question and described my experience, and when he did not dismiss it, I knew I had found the right person. I spent about eighteen months in analytic therapy, working with dreams and fantasies, drawing and writing, using every technique in his repertoire to rediscover my *anima* and to tame her from tormentor to spiritual ally. Slowly I began to see that my intellect, my conscious self, is no more that a cork bobbing on the sea of the unconscious, sometimes pacific and sometimes roiling, and that this domain of the heart was presented to me in to form of the awe-ful, frightening, yet somehow supremely attractive, old woman. In the forty years since, I have been probing her lesson.

I also somehow connected this vision with the place where it had occurred, in Bouddhanath, amid the richly symbolic Tibetan Tantric tradition it embodies. I read W. Y. Evens-Wentz's edition of *The Tibetan Book of the Dead,* one of the most stimulating books I have ever encountered. As I read, I vowed that someday I would read it in the original Tibetan, and I have. In fact, I eventually taught an entire college course about this esoteric masterpiece.

During this period of study, I also thoroughly enjoyed John Blofeld's *The Tantric Mysticism of Tibet*, and even wrote a fan letter to the author. Much to my surprise, he sent me a lovely and lengthy handwritten response, and we kept up a correspondence for years. Eventually we met, and I even visited him in his Bangkok home several times. Although tall and fair-skinned, John somehow struck one as Chinese. It was not only his native fluency in the language or his preference for wearing a wrinkled Chinese silk jacket, it was the way he carried himself with the elegance of a Chinese gentleman. Somehow, his interior life imprinted itself onto his very demeanor, and he retained an impishness that was completely disarming. We once traveled around China together. When it was time for our tour group to visit the Great Wall, he said, "It is indeed a great wall, but a wall is only a wall, no matter how great. Let's hire a taxi and I will take you to some of the haunts of my youth here." And so we did. From Taoist temple, to serene wooded park, to a three-hundred-year-old Chinese barbecue restaurant, that day ranks among my most memorable travel experiences. My friendship with John is one of the treasures of my life.

But the most striking book I read was H. V. Guenther's *The Life and Teachings of Naropa*, a hagiographic biography of an Indian Tantric master. In particular, the description of the master's encounter with his *anima* (*dakini* in Sanskrit, *khendroma* in Tibetan) was an exact model of what I had experienced in Bouddhanath. So I found the answer to my mystery through two divergent sources, Jungian psychology and Tantric Buddhism. I was so inspired by my discovery that I wrote a paper about it for a graduate seminar on psychology and religion. It is one of the best pieces I have ever written, and even after thirty-five years I am proud of it.[1] It has been translated into a number of languages and republished in several anthologies and books. Most of my academic colleagues may learn for the first time when they read this that my academic musings are deeply rooted in mystical experience. I wonder what they will think.

Life After the *Dakini*

My experience with the *dakini* changed my life, and if I ever need to "prove" to myself that she was no ordinary dream, I need only look at the con-

---

[1] "Anima and mKha' 'gro ma: A Critical, Comparative Study of Jung and Tibetan Buddhism," *Tibet Journal* 2/3 (1977): 13–43.

sequences. She led me to psychotherapy, which has been deeply useful in my personal life, and to a commitment to meditation and spirituality. I learned that the inner soul, the *anima*, can be either a haunting demon, as the *dakini* seemed to be, or an angelic comfort, depending on how well one knows her. Like a crying baby, the more one tries to avoid her, the louder she cries, but the moment one cradles her in his arms, she becomes calm and exudes love. She also led me to a career as an academic, and that, at any rate, is no dream!

She also instilled in me a passion for Indian and Tibetan culture. What had been repugnant became attractive. I now feel grateful for the spirit I once hated. India, the place that so appalled me, has come to be one of my three spiritual homes, along with Israel and America.

And she has been the *leitmotif* of my inner life, of balancing the outer, rational male *persona* with the inner, intuitive *anima*. Just as for historical reasons Judaism moved from the priestly sacrificial system of the Temple to the home and its dining table, so my own life has made a similar redirection from exterior to interior.

3

The Sixties Spiritual Salad Bar
Philadelphia

～

Jewish tradition clearly demarcates the stages of human development, and it does so differently for girls and boys. The Sages of Israel compare a boy toddler to a sapling tree whose fruit may not be plucked until it has grown for three years. Just as the tree remained untouched until it had matured enough for the ancients to bring its first fruit (*bikkurim*) to the Holy Temple as a sacrifice, so the boy's hair stays unshorn until his third birthday. At the *Opshern* hair-cutting ceremony, the shaggy child sings, "The Torah was given us through Moses, a heritage for the community of Jacob." The father or the rabbi then presents the child with a chart or a book with the Hebrew alphabet on which some honey has been smeared, and the boy laps up the honey, symbolically being taught that learning is sweet. This is when his education traditionally commences. After his *Opshern*, the boy is considered a "youth" (*na'ar*), and he is taught the rudiments of Hebrew and religious observance.

Much better known is the bar-mitzvah, when once again the boy, now thirteen, undertakes a ritual performance, typically reading from the Torah or perhaps leading the prayer liturgy, after which he is considered a morally responsible agent. He continues his education in both religious and secular subjects, and ideally, by the time of his marriage he is prepared for both earning a livelihood and fully participating in a life of prayer and advanced study.

My bar-mitzvah in 1961 was, to be honest, an unpleasant ordeal. I was haunted by my inability to carry a tune, and my youthful passion for prayer had faded as I entered my teen years of hormones and rebelliousness. I resisted learning more of the Torah cantillation than I absolutely had to. I became unruly in Hebrew school. When my big day came, I rushed through my performance, wincing as my voice cracked, and feeling more embarrassment than pride. During this rite of passage, I was much more focused on getting over an ordeal than on bathing in the light that had illuminated my synagogue experiences just a few years before. My pubescent awkwardness made me fear the elaborate party my parents had planned. My rented tuxedo did not fit, and I worried whether girls would want to dance with me even at my own party.

The event coincided with a broader cultural shift from the conformist fifties to the rebellious sixties. The natural rhythms of my personal development reflected the coming of age of the notorious baby boom generation. In short, I was a child during the fifties and a teenager during the sixties. May Hashem have mercy on my poor parents!

Poetry at Temple University

As a Camden boy, I grew up in the shadow of Walt Whitman, one of America's greatest mystical poets as well as a local hero. He was everywhere: the Walt Whitman movie theater, Walt Whitman High School, the Walt Whitman Hotel. where my bar-mitzvah reception was held, Whitman's Chocolates, and later the Walt Whitman Bridge, which connected Camden with South Philadelphia. Even in primary school, we were taught some of his work. I took to it with a passion, and poetry became another of life's pleasures for me. So I declared a major in English when I entered Temple University, and I took all the poetry classes I could. I also loved theater, and read everything I could from Shakespeare to Ionesco, and even acted in several productions, including taking the role of the professor in *The Lesson*.

Poetry blended with my interest in mysticism, especially the work of William Blake. Poetry also blended with my rebelliousness, so I loved Allen Ginsberg. I wished I had the courage to emulate his defiance of all authority, civil or moral, as well as the unflinching, painful honesty of his self-revealing (some would say exhibitionistic) poems, and his witty sarcasm. I came to know him when we were both members of the core faculty at Naropa Institute. A few years later, when I was on the faculty of Williams College, I was able to bring Allen in for a reading. In fact, he was the first guest at our new home in the Berkshires. I remember introducing him to a large crowd. I said that I was convinced that the spirit of Blake had reincarnated in Whitman, who in turn reincarnated in Ginsberg. The audience laughed appreciatively, and I was surprised that Allen had never heard of such a possibility.

An Interfaith Zoo

My mysticism drew me to courses in Temple's fine religion department. In those days, the founding chair of the department, Bernard Phillips, a Jewish Zen-Sufi, implemented his vision for the academic study of religion by hiring scholar-practitioners for his faculty. I loved it, and if I had not already completed my English major requirements, I would have shifted to religion. I contented myself with a minor.

I learned about Hinduism from the esteemed Swami Nikhilananda, head of the Ramakrishna Order in New York City, as well as from Jehangir Chubb, a disciple of the evolutionary Hindu thinker Sri Aurobindo. In those days during the sixties, some three hundred students attended the swami's classes. Swamiji was as inspiring as Chubb was tough-minded, and I began to appreciate both the fuzzy mysticism and the rigorous analytical approaches of Hindu traditions.

My professor of Judaism was Robert Gordis, a wonderful scholar of Bible from the Jewish Theological Seminary of America. The professor who influenced me the most was Maurice Friedman, a disciple of Martin Buber. We maintain a friendship to this day, and Buber's dialogical philosophy touched me deeply.

I learned about Islam from the imposing Palestinian imam Isma'il al-Faruqi. A large and eloquent man, al-Faruqi had the uncanny ability to express the most radical ideas in the most charming style. In those days, Temple had a cooperative agreement with the Reconstructionist Rabbinical College, then just a few blocks north on Broad Street, and many of the RRC's rabbinical students simultaneously pursued a doctorate in religion. Many took Professor al-Faruqi's courses, and I felt that if soon-to-be-rabbis could embrace al-Faruqi's views, which were stridently anti-Zionist, then I could too. After all, I subscribed to the political wisdom of the day that the only thing required for peace in the Middle East was for Israel to be more accommodating of Palestinian aspirations. Besides, the imam was a charming gentleman who always had time for his students, and I considered him a friend.

To be frank, I was less interested in Christianity than in any other of the world's religions, and never took a course in it, although Temple had some fine scholars in the field. To this day, I probably know less about this, the largest religion in the world, than any other.

A Korean Zen monk who was also pursuing his Ph.D., the Venerable Kyung-bo Seo, taught Buddhism. Dr. Seo's classes met at 8:00 a.m. on Tuesdays and Thursdays, and even in the morning haze of the sixties, I hardly ever was late for class. In retrospect, I guess that Dr. Seo was more practitioner than scholar, which suited me just fine then. I still remember his discussion of the doctrine of the Three Bodies of a Buddha. His English was not great, and he told us that his was the body of a Buddha and that ours were the bodies of a Buddha. He walked over to the window and, gesturing at North Philadelphia's dreary sky, said, "This too is the body of Buddha." I had never quite seen North Philadelphia in that way before, but at that moment I did.

Dr. Seo established a *zendo*, a Zen meditation hall, in his very modest apartment in North Philadelphia, a very tough neighborhood. He was a small man who wore the gray robes of Korean Zen. His face bore a very stern expression that transformed into an effusive smile at the slightest provocation, or sometimes for no apparent reason at all. On Sunday mornings he taught meditation in his apartment, and I often attended. Among my classmates was a fellow who became the president of the Zen Center of Los Angeles, one of the most esteemed Zen centers in North America. I took to the tough-minded practice of sitting on a cushion (*zafu*) with back straight, tongue firmly implanted against the teeth, and breathing to and from the diaphragm. Certainly discipline was not one of the higher virtues in sixties culture, but I guess we did seek it out somewhat, as it is a basis for most mystical practices. I struggled to observe my thoughts without trying either to repress them or follow them, and I welcomed the rap on my back from Dr. Seo's zen stick, used skillfully to return the mind to the breath when it strayed into thought.

One Sunday each month, Dr. Seo would host a picnic in Philadelphia's expansive Fairmount Park. Somewhere I read that more of Philadelphia's total area is dedicated to parkland than any other city's. I do not know if this is true, but Fairmount Park is certainly huge, varied, and beautiful. All Philadelphians know this and love the park, but I felt that I had never truly seen it before I experienced it with Dr. Seo and his Zen attitude. Dr. Seo and a number of us would slowly walk the park's hilly trails, like so many baby ducks following their mother. Suddenly he would stop, the group of us nearly bumping each other's backs. We'd gather round to better hear his words at the moment it seemed he was about to speak. "Very pretty place," was all he said, and somehow we were able to gaze at the beauty through his eyes, and the park, beautiful as it was, became so much more so.

Professor Phillips's experiment in creating a department of scholar-practitioners was generally not very well respected in the academic world, as I would learn years later. The chair of the religion department at Temple's crosstown rival, the University of Pennsylvania, authored a report on the field with a scathing assessment of Temple's program. He called it the "zoo theory" approach to the study of religion, with professors' offices likened to the animal cages in a zoo. Unfortunately, the characterization stuck, and after Professor Philips's untimely passing, the junior members of the department did everything in their power to unravel his vision. By the time I returned for graduate studies, Temple's department had reinvented itself along more traditional, purely academic lines. Like most university programs in the study of religion, Temple's had become long on academics but short on experience, an inversion of the aspirations that had brought me back for graduate school.

Gurus Galore

In Professor Phillips's department, guest lectures by nearly every imaginable guru were on the table. I remember a talk by Swami Bhaktivedanta, founder of the International Society for Krishna Consciousness, popularly known as the Hare Krishna movement. Bhaktivedanta was a stern-minded man, and I was frankly put off by his dogmatism at the same time that I was attracted by the ecstasy induced by the practice of *kirtan*, or chanting the names of God. Bhaktivedanta also struck me as moralistic, and I asked him in all sincerity what was wrong with the concept of "free love" that was pervasive in sixties culture. Seated in the lotus posture, the generally unsmiling swami's steely eyes glared at me with even more sternness. Let us just say that his response was not particularly respectful of my point of view.

I was, as we used to say, turned off, but at that same lecture, one of my classmates, William Deadwiler, met Bhaktivedanta for the first time and seemed to know in an instant that he had found his guru. I could not imagine what it was that he saw in him, but Bill became head of the Philadelphia Krishna temple, and he is one of the world leaders of the movement. A keenly intelligent, upright fellow, Bill often welcomed my students when I brought classes to the Krishna temple as part of a world religions course.

On one occasion some years later, Bill invited my dissertation adviser, Professor Bibhuti Yadav, to meet the swami, so we went, along with one or two more of Yadav's students. It was an ugly scene. Although to this day I am not entirely sure why, Bhaktivedanta felt that Yadav had somehow disrespected him and bade him to leave under threat. We scurried out, and Yadav was visibly shaken by the encounter.

On another occasion, the Sikh meditation teacher Sant Kirpal Singh gave a public class at the leading downtown hotel, the Bellevue Stratford, later famous as the home of Legionnaires' Disease. Of course, I went. The Sant, like many Punjabis, was a tall man, and his military-like posture made him seem all the more imposing, as did his elegant blue turban, long white beard, and flowing white kurta-pyjama, typical North Indian dress. He led the meditation with surprisingly little instruction, and it was pleasant enough. After meditating, the Sant took out a little notebook and conducted a survey of what color lights we had seen with our mind's eyes while meditating. I think my lights were blue, and he seemed avidly interested in the color of these inner lights, feverishly taking notes as many people in the audience described their experiences. After hearing from everyone, he tucked his notebook into the pocket of his kurta and took his leave with no explanation. To this day, I haven't a clue what all that meant.

Another of the gurus of the day, the leader of the Western Sufi Order, Pir Vilayat Khan, came to town with his gentle dancing, a tame version of the energetic whirling I was later to learn from Sufis in Afghanistan. The Pir was an extremely mild soul, and his mind seemed able to penetrate others' with remarkable skill. Not surprisingly, several of my friends became disciples on the spot, and today they occupy high positions in Western Sufism.

The exchanges between these gurus and their would-be disciples sometimes demonstrated the immensity of the cultural chasms between them. One woman asked the Pir his view of abortion rights, assuming he would offer comfort. Instead, he replied that abortion was the one sin that was truly unforgivable. The audience, certain of the correctness of their opinions, was palpably shocked.

One day, one of my fellow students brought Rabbi Shlomo Carlebach to Maury Friedman's comparative mysticisms seminar. Reb Shlomo had a marvelous singing voice and, accompanying himself on the guitar, led us in several of the wordless melodies known as *niggunim* that are a central part of Hasidic worship.

In the 1950s, Reb Shlomo and Rabbi Zalman Schachter, who was to figure prominently in my path, were sent by their rebbe, the late Rabbi Yosef Yitzchak Schneerson, the previous Lubavitcher Rebbe, to be his emissaries to college and university students across North America. Shlomo and Zalman traveled the country bringing the Rebbe's message of love and spirituality to one and all. Shlomo founded the House of Love and Prayer, one of the cornerstones of the remarkable Haight-Ashbury scene in San Francisco during the fabled Summer of Love of 1967.

Shlomo was also a musical genius; the melodies he composed for the Jewish liturgy have since become so standard in synagogues worldwide that most congregants assume they have been sung this way for centuries. His melodies are uncanny in their simplicity and depth. They somehow become ingrained in the listener's memory and soul after just one hearing. Those tunes powerfully elevate the soul, precisely because of their profound simplicity.

Shlomo was also a very gregarious person. He embraced every student in the classroom with a bear hug and a belly laugh, dispelling any reticence, or "uptightness" as we used to put it. Years later I learned to my dismay that Shlomo had indeed embraced far too many people in less than appropriate ways, yet his spiritual music was so powerful, so deep, that he has not been dismissed by the Orthodox Jewish world. Indeed, many of today's newly observant Jews, or *baalei-teshuvah*, made their way to Judaism through Shlomo.

Many others passed through Philadelphia: Baba Ram Dass né Richard Alpert, had dinner in the communal house where I lived at the time. Brilliant and witty, prone to ecstasy by any means available, Ram Dass exuded the era's characteristic hedonistic spirituality.

Everyone came through town: Swami Muktananda, who taught the esoteric breathing technique called *kundalini,* said to awaken a serpentine spiritual power that travels up and down the spinal cord, transforming eros into Divine love; Yogi Bhajan, a jolly Sikh who ran the vegetarian food concessions at countless rock festivals; Philip Kapleau Roshi, a Jewish Zen master of sharp intellect and serious demeanor; and Dr. Timothy Leary, who despite countless LSD trips never ceased being a horny barroom jokester. I learned to cast astrological charts and consult the *I Ching;* I read Gurdjieff, practiced yoga, and even considered UFO cults like the one covered in the Urantia book and the channeling of Edgar Cayce. I became friendly with a fellow resident of a decrepit Powelton Village apartment building aptly called "The Piles," local guru Ira Einhorn, who later became infamous as a trunk murderer! I joined psychological encounter groups and, given my theatrical interests, became involved with psychodrama, as well as my own Jungian analytical therapy.

I felt that I learned from each of them. My American individualism meant that any synthesis or combination of mysticisms had to be of my own design to be valid. In precisely this sense, the spiritual salad bar of the sixties was very much the precursor of today's contemporary spirituality in America and elsewhere.

Sixties Culture and Politics

Both culture—rock and roll especially—and the politics of the New Left were as much part of the sixties as mystical eclecticism. One of my older friends opened a penny-candy store inside Philadelphia's rock mecca, the Electric Factory. We took turns staffing the cubicle-sized store, selling gumballs or wax mustaches to stoned-out revelers who had the munchies. The best part was that the parade of rock bands was no less extensive than the parade of gurus, and I saw Janis Joplin, the Grateful Dead, Electric Flag, Cream, the Fugs, the Mothers of Invention, the Byrds, Quicksilver Messenger Service, and the list goes on. Many years later, my wife, Ellen Goldberg, and I hosted a radio program, *The Sixties Show,* on a community radio station in Tampa. My scratchy old vinyl discs and our half-baked political commentary were the show's mainstay.

Politics was also an essential part of the sixties. In many senses, the decade's culture was born out of the civil rights movement and opposition to the Vietnam War. Many of us in love beads and paisley shirts had been inspired by the Rev. Dr. Martin Luther King's example. Youths are by nature impatient, and I felt his "I Have a Dream Speech" should have settled the issues of civil rights forever. How could anyone not join in when right and wrong were so obvious? Like many of my fellow students, I felt so profound a sense of disillusionment that racism persisted after 1964, and that economic and social disparities remained, that I rejected gradual, democratic change, and became radicalized.

Coming from Camden, quite naturally I identified with these aspirations. But quite a few years later, at a high school class reunion in 1981, I was amazed to discover that many of my classmates were conservative Reaganites. I had underestimated, as do many liberals, the conservatism that pervades a fair chunk of the African-American community. Self-discipline, a strong family, education, and faith mattered to them, as they did to many of my classmates, and as they do to many white evangelical Christians and most people in my Orthodox community today. I guess I continued to value my old friends' opinions, and they made me rethink many of my assumptions.

Back in the sixties, however, right and wrong were stark. They certainly were clear to us when it came to the war in Vietnam. We bought into the characterization of the United States as an imperial tormentor of indigenous peoples, and we identified with the Vietnamese in their struggle against us. This identification, incidentally, led some of us to idealize Vietnam's culture uncritically, including its Buddhist faith, thus linking the political with the cultural. What's more, I began to accept the leftist perception of Israel as a surrogate for America, with the Palestinians as analogs to the Vietnamese. It took quite a few years and a lot of on-the-spot experience to extirpate this naive understanding.

At the time, I felt I had convenient, ready-made answers to every possible question. Today, I see my sixties self as simultaneously idealistic and narcissistic. I believed what I sincerely felt to be right, but I also believed what was convenient and self-justifying. How all too easy it was to avoid not only military service, but also anything that imposed limits on our excesses, and to feel virtuous all the while. Sex, drugs, and rock and roll. While I look back on myself as a cliché, I also don't want to be too harsh. I *was,* at least to some extent, serious, certainly about rediscovering both the light that had shone from my childhood Ark and the deep sense of community that had been destroyed. Finding both has just taken me much longer than I anticipated, and I had to travel a circuitous route I could not possibly have envisioned.

4

Mullas in the City, Sufis in the Mountains
Kabul

~

Haunted by my vision in Nepal and fortified by my studies of eastern religions and my analytical therapy, I set off again for Asia as soon as I graduated at the end of 1970. My readings had tantalized me, and I was all set to learn Tibetan and be enlightened.

I booked passage for Morocco on a Yugoslav freighter and set off even before my graduation ceremony. Crossing the North Atlantic was rough, but after thirteen tempest-tossed days I alighted in Tangiers not much worse for the ride. With Crosby, Stills, and Nash in my brain, I boarded the Marrakech Express (literally) to Marrakech, where I bought a 1958 VW microbus and toured that beautiful country for a month. Living was cheap, and the few thousand dollars I had managed to save was a fortune. I visited old synagogues in Fez and Meknes, trekked in the High Atlas Mountains, managed to get down to the fringes of the Sahara, and ate fresh Atlantic fish at Essouara. On board the ship, I had met a follower of Subud, an Indonesian Islamic esoteric sect. He referred me to his coreligionists in the American military near Rabat, so I sought them out and learned about their Latihan system of meditation and divination. I lay on a military-issue cot, as instructed, and felt the twinges of divination in my left shoulder, also as suggested, but was unable to discover any particular value to these quirky experiences.

Then I set out on the great overland trek. I meandered from campground to campground up and down Europe, across Turkey and Iran. By the time I reached Afghanistan some months later, my money was running low. But luck was with me. I was fortunate to land a job with the United States Information Agency teaching English in Afghanistan. I ended up spending the better part of two years there.

I think it is not uncommon for people to develop a special fondness for the first foreign country in which they reside. Certainly that happened to me in Afghanistan. Absolutely everything was exciting. I threw myself into learning Dari, the Persian dialect of the region. Each morning my tutor, Baz Mohammed, would come by and we would have an hour's lesson over eggs, tea, and nan (an arrowhead-shaped flat bread made of whole wheat in Afghanistan, where it is much heartier and tastier than the pale version in Indian restaurants). Then, as I walked to work at the American Center, I would practice my lesson for the day with shopkeepers. Everyone was patient with me, apparently pleased by my efforts to learn their language. Within nine or ten months I could converse easily, and a few months later I could even appreciate some of the beauties of Persian Sufi poetry. Indeed, I have never learned another spoken language as well as I learned Dari, but it has been many years and, as they would say, most of the words *az yadem raft*, "have flown out of my head."

Baz became not only my language tutor, but also my closest Afghan friend and cultural guide. He accompanied me on many of my sojourns around the country, at times guiding the old VW across trails with only a compass and a prayer.

I was most fond of a region in the central part of the country known for two remarkable sights: Bamiyan and Band-I-Amir. The world today knows about Bamiyan because it is where the Taliban ignoramuses, who later ran the country, felt the need to destroy two colossal Buddha statues. Once a crossroads on the silk route, Bamiyan was famous for its huge Buddhist monastery, with a formidable library and thousands of monks' cells carved out of a sandstone cliff, the same palisade out of which the Buddhas were carved. When I visited, it was still possible to ascend hidden stairways and sit right on the statues' heads, enjoying a spectacular view of the fertile valley surrounded by tan desert, and imagining the view to be just a tad akin to the Buddha's vision, seeing directly out of his eyes, as it were.

Soon after the Arab Muslim conquest of Afghanistan during the seventh century, religious zealots had cut off the faces of the statues; such was their abhorrence of idolatry. I guess zealotry has increased over the centuries, because the Taliban felt that defacing was not good enough—even though, according to Islamic law, all one has to do to make an idol inoffensive is to make a small cut on its nose or ear—so they detonated the statues despite outcries from around the world, including from most Muslim judges. The Taliban didn't treat the women of Afghanistan much better than they did these silent stone commemorations to wisdom and compassion.

Band-I-Amir is less known to the outside world, probably because it is less easy to demolish lakes. This low valley holds seven interconnecting lakes, and the soil's extremely rich mineral content makes for gaudy colors all along the rims of the lakes, one lower than the next. As soon as I arrived, hot and dusty from the drive, I dove into the nearest lake only to virtually fly back out to the shore, so cold was the water. There is not a more inspiring and beautiful spot on our planet.

One time, Baz and I went to Jelalabad, in the Pashtu-dominated eastern part of the country. The drive from Kabul to Jelalabad is one of the most majestic, and dangerous, in the world. One proceeds through the Kabul Gorge, whose stark, dramatic cliffs soar thousands of feet above the rushing Kabul River. It is as inspiring as America's Grand Canyon, but virtually unknown to the outside world. Jelalabad itself is between the Kabul Gorge and the Khyber Pass, which divides Afghanistan from Pakistan. Jelalabad's mild climate is hospitable to luxuriant orange groves.

We stayed with some Peace Corps volunteers in town, and one of their neighbors hosted a wedding to which we were invited. Drums accompanied the oud-like Afghan stringed instrument, the *rhobab*, to create the musical background for a remarkable show. Transvestite barbers provided the entertainment. "In Pashtunistan," Baz explained to me, "only the barbers dance." In a display of Afghan hospitality, the father of the bride offered me any of the dancers I fancied. I stumbled for a moment and lied, "Thank you, brother, but I am already married." My attempt at a polite refusal didn't exactly work. With utter befuddlement on his face, he asked how that could possibly matter. "Women are for having children," he said with an expansive gesture, "but a boy is for pleasure." Although the music was pleasant and the food good, I left soon thereafter.

I taught English daily to students who had been selected for various scholarships or training programs in America, and got to know many of them personally. Hospitality is a central cultural value in Afghanistan, and I was invited frequently for meals and holidays, weddings and festivals. I even picnicked at the king's private farm, thanks to a princess who was my student. I also let it be known that I was interested in Sufism, and a few like-minded students offered to take me to some of the country's great *shuyukh* (mystical teachers).

A rich folk tradition surrounds Sufi *shuyukh* (plural of *shaikh*). They are said to appear and disappear, tantalizing and testing would-be disciples. So more often than not, we would drive for hours, sometimes for days, hire a cart or a camel, and then hike up a mountain, only to find that the sought-after *shaikh* had just left, or had just died, or was too busy to see us. All part of the mysticism. But on occasion we would find him sipping green tea, and happy to receive and teach us. I especially recall a few days spent at one of the holiest shrines in the country, Mazar-I-Sharif, the "Noble Tomb," dedicated to the Caliph Ali. There were Sufis galore, and I spent the time learning the energetic meditative practice known as *dhikr*, the recitation of Qur'anic verses or names of Allah, all while vigorously swaying and prostrating. The simultaneous results of an hour or two of this practice are physical exhaustion and spiritual exaltation. I felt propelled into a divine realm.

Since my American supervisors perceived me as particularly sensitive to Islam, I got the assignment to teach English to the faculty of Islamic law (Shari'a) at Kabul University. Once or twice a week an embassy driver would take me to the campus, where I would give the English lesson and then sit around and discuss religion, philosophy, and mysticism with the *mullali*, some of the country's leading religious authorities. My Dari was better than their English, so we talked at length in Dari, especially about analogs between Islam and Judaism. I only wish I had known more about Jewish law at the time, because it would have been of the greatest interest to my hosts.

The professor with whom I developed the closest relationship was the head of the Shari'a department, Imam Burhanuddin Rabbani. He was an erudite gentleman, keenly interested in the religions of the world. We had any number of extended conversations, and we developed a friendly relationship. Years later, he resurfaced as a leader of the Afghan resistance movement known in American newspapers as the Northern Alliance. I wrote to him offering congratulations when he became president of Afghanistan in 1992, but either my letter never reached him or he had more pressing matters on his mind.

I also on occasion attended the synagogue on "Chicken Street," just across from the Saudi embassy, but my faint efforts at connecting with my heritage were not much more successful in Afghanistan than they had been in the United States. I did, however, make some friends in Kabul's four-hundred-family Jewish community. In those days, being a Jew in that part of the Muslim world was not a problem. Jews were cousins, Muslims told me again and again, and I never experienced anything but respect, hospitality, and friendship.

Sometimes, craving the sight of greenery, I would steal away for brief vacations in northern Pakistan, now the center of al-Qaeda's miserable world. Just thirty-five years ago, the soul-destroying anti-Semitism that infects so much of the Muslim world today was pretty much unknown. Now and then, the question of the Israeli-Palestinian conflict would arise, and the most commonly voiced opinion I heard was that the problem was far removed from Afghanistan and no one seemed to care much about it.

While living in Kabul, I received a telephone call one Monday morning with the news that my father had died. My mind raced. My relationship with my father had been a troubled one, but I knew that he admired my life in Afghanistan. Stories of childhood in the Ukraine were my reference points as I encountered bearded mullas, horse-drawn carts, cup after cup of chai, mud streets with open sewers, and open-air abattoirs. To my mind, Kabul of the 1970s was like Dinowitz of the 1910s, and my father had told me how much he enjoyed my descriptive letters that brought his childhood back to him. I felt that he approved of my adventures, an approval that I felt had been absent almost all of my life, because in some way Afghanistan was different.

My own voice pulled me back from my reverie as I heard myself yelling into the telephone that I would somehow manage to get back by Friday, and that my family should schedule the funeral before Shabbat, as Halakhah requires. When I hung up the phone, my grief was mixed with surprise that at this crucial moment, my thoughts were about Jewish law. It was the last thing I would have expected, and it made me wonder what lay beneath the surface of my consciousness. Obviously, there was more than I knew.

I was indeed home by Friday, but I soon returned to Kabul, unsure about my future. Since my two-year commitment to the American Center was drawing to a close, I pondered what to do next. The USIA offered me a position directing a similar English language institute in Indonesia. I gave a lot of thought to pursuing a career in English as a second language education, and even applied to a graduate program in the field. However, my love of eastern religions still drove me, so I also applied to Temple University's doctoral program in religion. When Temple accepted me, I took that path, but before I returned to the States, I set off for India to start learning Tibetan and Sanskrit in preparation for my graduate studies. I left Kabul in my creaky, noisy VW, traveling through the Khyber Pass, destined first for the Himalayan kingdom of Sikkim.

5

Visualizing the Buddha
Gangtok, Sikkim

~

I am not sure which was more intimidating. Here I was, a twenty-four-year-old soon-to-be graduate student who was trying to learn Tibetan in a small institute in Sikkim in the eastern Himalayas—in other words, nobody at all. A regally bedecked elephant greeted the diplomatic Mercedes-Benz in which I was riding as it pulled up at the cavernous Ashoka Hotel, then the finest in New Delhi. Having become accustomed to "budget" hotels (I am using the word kindly) in Afghanistan and India, the Ashoka's commanding edifice was alien and frightening. My purpose in coming was even more imposing than the elephant or the Mercedes. I was to meet His Holiness, the Fourteenth Dalai Lama of Tibet. But I am getting ahead of myself.

It's not that I was unfamiliar with esteemed lamas. Sure, I had become friendly with the Sixteenth Gwalya Karmapa at his regal quarters at Rumtek Monastery in Sikkim. Even in those days, a visit to Sikkim just wasn't complete without calling on its most esteemed lama, and he seemed to take a ready liking to me. The Karmapa held the longest-established lineage of "living Buddhas," or *tulkus*, in all Tibet, and was regarded as one of the greatest spiritual masters of all Buddhism. His round face was often in a scowl that would transform itself at the slightest provocation into a huge smile with deep laughter. He wore the silks of a prince, sat on a Dharma throne, and conducted his affairs in the style of a maharaja in his *darbar*, or public court.

And yes, I had studied with the energetic teacher of the Nyingma Order, Dodrup Chen Rinpoche, who seemed always to be busily making notes about his countless projects, and engaging in rapid exchanges with petitioners who came to him in an endless stream of supplications for mystic intervention into their problems.

But this was the Dalai Lama, Tibet's greatest luminary. I was nervous, scared.

Help from the Maharani

For the past several months I had been studying Tibetan in Gangtok, Sikkim, at the Namgyal Institute of Tibetology, named for the erstwhile royal family. This was in fulfillment of my heart's desire. In part because of my experiences in Nepal several years before, in part because I had devoured everything I could find in English about Tibetan Buddhism, and in part because of my undergraduate studies in religion at Temple University, I had decided that the only way to really understand this dazzling spiritual tradition was to read its texts in Tibetan, and to learn about them from their masters.

My undergraduate mentor, Dr. Maurice Friedman, had imposed upon his former student at Sarah Lawrence College, Hope Namgyal née Cook, to sponsor me in her tiny country. She had led the seemingly storybook life of a privileged American girl who met and married the crown prince of Sikkim. At the time of the royal wedding, she had become something of a celebrity in America, akin to Jordan's Queen Noor, with the important proviso that Sikkim is no Jordan. It is no longer even a country. Professor Friedman had written to the maharani, asking her to facilitate my studies there. It was no easy process, even with the backing of the royal family, but eventually the Indian powers that oversaw the protectorate of Sikkim from New Delhi granted permission. At the beginning of 1973, I ensconced myself at the institute's very modest hostel and began my studies.

Some problems had arisen with my residency permit, so I had to journey all the way to New Delhi to sort things out. I was staying at the YMCA, and one morning I received a phone call from Tashi Densapa, a scion of Sikkim's royal family who had befriended me. "How would you like to meet the Dalai Lama?" he asked. I didn't need a second invitation. "When?" was my only response, and he said, "Today. I will pick you up at ten o'clock.

I spruced up as best I could. The official Sikkimese Mercedes rolled up, and off I went, nerves aflutter. What could I say to someone like the Dalai Lama? I guessed that there really was no one like the Dalai Lama, and the thought only increased my anxiety.

It seemed miles down the hotel's huge corridor as we approached his suite. My hands trembled and my palms were sweaty as I fumbled with the long white silk scarf known as a *katha*, which Tibetans use as a token of greeting. After I waited a short while, the Dalai Lama entered the anteroom. I rose and fumbled with the scarf some more. Seeing my distress, the Dalai Lama broke up into a hearty belly laugh in his deep, mellifluous voice. He briefly touched the scarf, brushed it aside, and gave me a hearty handshake. Just that quickly, my nervousness dissipated. I knew I was in for something very, very special. In fact, this relationship has turned out to be one of the most important in my life.

For whatever reasons, we seemed to hit it off and spent much of the day together. He asked me why I wanted to study Tibetan, what my goals were. Audaciously, I told him that I wanted to undertake a comparative study of Tantric Buddhism and Kabbalah—not that I knew more than a tad about either at the time, but he seemed interested and was certainly encouraging.

I had intuited parallels in the metaphysics, or theologies, of the two esoteric systems. I was intrigued by their extravagant use of male/female symbolism, indicating a "divine polarity" as some scholars put it. I was also intrigued by each movement's revaluation of its own traditions to experience the empirical, or physical, world as the expression of divinity, rather than as its opposite.

After chatting over tea, he invited me to join him and his entourage for a mass conversion ceremony where more than ten thousand "untouchables" embraced Buddhism, rejecting the Hindu society that they believed oppressed them. Part of the ceremony known as "taking refuge" in the Buddha, his Teachings, known as the Dharma, and his community, or the Sangha, was the renunciation of their familiar gods. As he instructed them to renounce other refuges, I could see pain on their faces. They may have wanted to step outside of the caste system, but perhaps not all wanted to reject their beloved and feared deities.

Visualizations

Returning to Gangtok, I threw myself into my work. I was assigned a dreary, damp room in the institute's hostel, and one of the staff brought me food. Most of the day was spent with language lessons and library readings, but I also was able to learn about a new and especially powerful form of Tantric meditation.

Just a short walk beyond the institute lay the *chorten*, a reliquary and home for the distinguished Nyingma teacher Dodrup Chen Rinpoche. He seemed always to have projects demanding his attention, but he also had time for practicing and teaching advanced meditation.

I learned that Dodrup Chen held the lineage of Longchen Nyingthig, or the essence of the teachings of the revered and creative master Longchenpa. With a small group of students, we began to learn a text that had been composed by a previous manifestation of Dodrup Chen. It opened the door to the quintessentially Tantric practice of visualization, also known as *deity yoga*.

This teaching is found in *sadhana* (practice) texts such as the one we were using. The *sadhana* is an especially vivid description of one of the Tibetan pantheon's myriad deities, which are explained as aspects of the enlightened mind. Depending on the personality and character of the practitioner, a deity is selected as the object of the meditation. The reason why a teacher assigns a particular deity to a particular student is complex and involves Tibetan systems akin to Jung's personality types. An aggressive person might be given a fierce-looking deity, whereas an especially compassionate aspirant might be assigned the Medical Buddha, for example. Some aspect of the student's personality that needs development is selected and symbolized.

A *sadhana* text describes the iconography of the deity in great detail, spelling out how many arms, what objects are held in each hand, colors, expressions, gestures of the hands, and so on. A *mantra*, a sacred phrase or sentence, is associated with the deity, and the letters of the *mantra* are placed like a caption in the description. As the text is read, the student is to visualize each detail of the deity, right down to the letters of the *mantra*. Once the student is able to picture mentally the deity described in the text, it is set into motion and given a voice. The deity dances and moves, the letters of the *mantra* scroll along like news headlines on television. Obviously, this takes enormous concentration, and I surprised myself when I was able to hold the mental picture for extended periods of time. This skill at constructing the mental image is called the "development phase" of the visualization meditation.

The mind-created deity speaks; the sounds of the *mantra* pervade the mind of the student. The deity also moves as if in a slow-motion dance of enlightenment, and finally the deity pours a chalice of *dudtsi*, or "nectar of immortality," *amrit* in Sanskrit, onto and into the head of the meditator. The inflow of *dudtsi* is accompanied by the dissolution of both the deity and the meditator, resulting in the sensation of the "great bliss"—a glimpse of egolessness, the infusion of the personality with a formless presence that Buddhists sometimes call *shunyata* (*töngpanyi*), and at other times call "the clear light" (*ösel*, or the highest reality).

Even then the thought crossed my mind: Is this the light of my childhood synagogue in Camden? Or is it something else?

In Tibetan culture, of course, the deities are known quantities. They are understood as aspects of enlightenment itself: compassion, or wisdom, or healing, or loving-kindness, or boundless energy, or peacefulness. By first mentally creating and then experientially identifying with these deities, the meditator is said to experience some enlightenment. When the ordinary personality dissolves along with the mind-created deity, all that is left is this *Shunyata*, this Clear Light, nondual and peaceful. This is called the "completion phase."

Rebellion in the Himalayas

Despite the Dalai Lama's blessing, my idyllic studies in Sikkim were near an end. I was invited to meet with the *chögyal*, Tibetan for "righteous monarch," the local term for the maharaja. Washing as best I could at an outdoor cold-water tap and donning my rumpled tweed suit, I made my way to his palace, perched atop the highest hill in Gangtok. Attired in colorful finery and swords, palace guards led me into a vast sitting room with crystal decanters filled with Scotch on silver trays, the finest Tibetan carpets, and priceless statues and paintings. The *chögyal* eventually appeared in a vested business suit, glass in his hand. He seemed bored as I replied to his polite question, and told him that I was enjoying the serenity of his fiefdom in the foothills. He scoffed over his drink. "You've got to be kidding. There is a revolution going on here!"

I had heard about some tensions, but I was naive enough to attribute his comment to the Scotch and to a desire to be provocative. But not even two weeks later, security guards came to my room and told me I had to leave for my own safety. Bewildered, I packed up my Volkswagen microbus, and the guards escorted me to the Indian border. I read later that the government of India had effectively seized Sikkim, which heretofore had been a protectorate, and within months it was declared a state within the Union of India. China made a few obligatory protests about Indian adventurism, but after its much more hostile takeover of Tibet, there was little to be said. The maharani returned to America, and the *chögyal* soon drank himself to death.

Learning in Dharamsala

About five years after meeting the Dalai Lama, during which time I had completed course work and defended my doctoral dissertation proposal back at Temple University (and it was not to be a comparison of Kabbalah and Tantra but a more pedestrian issue in Buddhist texts; I have yet to generate the *chutzpah* to give the extraordinarily complex project a shot), I was back in India. Supported by a Fulbright dissertation grant, I had settled myself in a hostel even more modest than the one in Gangtok; this one was attached to the Library of Tibetan Works and Archives in Dharamsala.

The library has the most extensive collection of Tibetan texts in the world, and Dharamsala is not only the seat of the Tibetan government-in-exile, but it is also the home in exile of the Dalai Lama. Gangtok was a delightful, bucolic town on the margin of the Tibetan exile culture; Dharamsala is its very heart. Situated atop a foothill with the Dhaulagiri Range as a backdrop and the lush Kangra Valley in the foreground, Dharamsala was a second-tier mountain resort in the British period. An occasional, dilapidated stone Anglican church seems out of place among even older Hindu temples and much more recently constructed Tibetan-style Buddhist monasteries. Two small parallel streets comprise the market area, dominated by a *chorten* (*stupa*, or reliquary) and prayer wheels repeatedly spun by pilgrims making the rounds. The market is replete with trinket sellers and little restaurants, above which the Dalai Lama's modest palace sits behind a small forest and many security guards.

Both the traditional and academic study of Buddhism make much of the distinctions between and among Buddhism's different forms. Most commonly, one speaks of the Inferior Vehicle (Hinayana), the Great Vehicle (Mahayana), and the Adamantine or Esoteric Vehicle (Vajrayana or Tantrayana). As a Jew, I found such ready and potentially demeaning terminology suspect. Just as the term "Old Testament" is the name of a Christian scripture that obviously overlaps with the Hebrew scripture, which traditional Jews call *Tanakh*,[1] so the term "Inferior Vehicle" set off alarm bells in me. If our text is not "old," I reasoned, then it is likely that the so-called Hinayana is not "inferior." My dissertation traced the notions of the ideal, perfected person in these three vehicles, to try to unearth the continuities among the myriad forms that Buddhism has taken at different times, in different places, and for different reasons.[2]

I had spent a year and a half from the middle of 1976 to the beginning of 1978 in Sri Lanka, working on the classical Pali language and the texts and practices of Theravada Buddhism, before coming to Dharamsala to read Sanskrit and Tibetan texts about both the ideal of Mahayana Buddhism, the *bodhisattva* or enlightenment-hero, and the *mahasiddha*, the wonder-working mystics of the Vajrayana. I was also attending Dharma classes that imparted something of the *bodhisattva* traditions to western students. These classes em-

---

[1] *Tanakh*, the Hebrew name for the Bible, is an acronym for *Torah* (the Five Books of Moses), *Nevi'im* (the Prophets), and *Ketubim* (miscellaneous writings, such as Lamentations, Song of Songs, and the Scroll of Esther).

[2] My dissertation was published as *Buddhist Images of Human Perfection* (Delhi: Motilal Banarsidass, 1982, 2nd ed. 1989).

phasized the practices of the *bodhisattva* path without neglecting the textual traditions on which those practices are based.

We were reading and practicing the *Entering the Path of the Bodhisattva* by the seventh-century Indian Buddhist saint Shantideva. This is still one of my favorite religious-spiritual texts, and I often teach it to my graduate students in seminars. The practices associated with this text involve a kind of self-denial as the basis for compassion, or valuing the other more than the self. "Whatever suffering there is in the world," Shantideva wrote, "comes about from pursuing one's own goals. Whatever happiness there is in the world comes about from pursuing the goals of others."

In Mahayana tradition, a practical application of this principle is known as "exchanging one's happiness for others' suffering." Having gone into a meditative state, one imagines one's happiness leaving on the out-breath and permeating others, while on the in-breath one takes in the sufferings of others. It is very powerful, a sharp technique for undercutting egoism and generating compassion.

This practice set the context for what was to come next. In reading over *mahasiddha* literature, I stumbled across a short text in the Tibetan canon known as the *Confession of Errors in the Roots and Branches of the Vajrayana*,[3] written by the Indian *pandit* Indrabhuti in the twelfth century. This struck me because all three forms of Buddhism have confession texts, all designed to spur the adept to higher and higher levels of practice and understanding. In the Theravada, the Pratimoksha literature confesses transgressions in the rules governing the austere lives of monks and nuns. In the *bodhisattva* traditions of the Mahayana, the aspirant for enlightenment confesses weaknesses in developing compassion, in egoism, and in pedagogic shortcomings. But here was a text of confessions about unskillful habits of mind, one of which is "regarding the human personality as inferior." This very life, Indrabhuti wrote, this very personality made up of five "aggregates of clinging," is in reality the five Buddha-families, aspects of enlightenment itself. In this stunning reversal, our Tantric master teaches that transcendence is here-and-now; enlightenment is not about rejecting our social or material selves, as earlier forms of Buddhism seemed to be teaching.

---

[3] "Indrabhuti's 'Confession of Errors in the Roots and Branches of the Vajrayana': A Critical Edition, English Translation and Discussion." *Journal of the International Association of Buddhist Studies* 2, no. 2 (1979): 31–44.

I can vividly recall walking up the steep mountainside from the library to Upper Dharamsala one day, perhaps to get a tastier meal than was available in the library's staff canteen. The two-mile walk was steep, but the view of Mount Dhaulagiri was inspiring. The pain in my calves blended with the snow-capped images before my eyes and the Dharma thoughts that lingered from the day's studies.

The impact of what I had been studying and practicing hit me as strongly as if I'd stepped right off snowcapped Dhaulagiri. "Enlightenment is here, not there," I thought.

To put this another way, the Alter Rebbe (the founder of Habad Hasidism, Rabbi Shneur Zalman) wrote in his seminal work, the *Tanya*, that the material is simply a disguise for the spiritual, and that our human task is to elevate the material or, to be more precise, to come to understand that the spiritual is the essence of the material.

I knew where I needed to go next, but it wasn't yet clear how to get there.

6

Becoming a Hindu in Benares

~

Kashi, "city of light" she is called. City of Shiva. Kashi Vishwanath. These are the names of Benares, Hinduism's most important pilgrimage center, where the faithful immerse themselves in Mata Ganga, the Mother of all Rivers, the Ganges, which flows from the very topknot of Lord Shiva's hair as he sits in meditative repose in the Himalayas.[1]

Truly, Benares is God's waiting room. From all over India, the elderly and infirm stream into the many *dharamshalas*, or hospices, to await the inevitable. When the time comes, the body is wrapped in a shroud and carried on a rattan stretcher to the banks of the Mother River, who is ready to receive her children with love. The body is washed, priests are hired, wood is purchased (and it is not cheap!), and the *samskaras* (life-cycle rituals) begin. As the priests chant verses from the *Vedas*, the pyre is lit. It takes about three hours to render most of the corpse into ash. Whatever is not burned is tossed into the River along with the ashes. Members of a special scavenger caste catch the remains, which they strain in large wicker baskets in search of any gold ornaments that the family felt too delicate to remove. The pyres burn day and night. It is not possible to gaze deeply into those pyres and not be changed by the experience.

A dawn or sunset stroll along the *ghats*—large steps leading from the town to the River—is one of life's memorable experiences. The ghats are something like the "riverwalks" found in many American cities today, with the significant difference that the *ghats* are three thousand or more years old! Amplified chants to Lord Ram or Shiva as Vishwanath (Lord of the Universe) are constant reminders of transcendence. Priests sit on platforms under large umbrellas to help pilgrims through the complex rites special to Benares. *Sadhus*—itinerant Hindu holy men—are plentiful. They wait in rows of saffron-clad opportunities for charity as pilgrims make their way down to the *ghats*. Occasionally

---

[1] This chapter is based on "Jerusalem in Benares," *Tikkun* (May/June 2007): 23–25, 68–70.

a *sadhu* breaks away from the crowd, erects a small altar to one of the many divine manifestations of Hinduism, lights a candle, and measures his prayers with a rosary of *neem* seeds. Meanwhile, buffalo, dogs, cows, and goats push their way through the crowds, making walking an exercise in focusing on the transcendent above and the archetypically mundane on the ground.

Every evening just after sunset, Mata Ganga is worshipped with chants and a fire ceremony known as *aarti*. Worshippers wave lamps in circles, accompanied by chanting, in homage to the deity. As one of my swami friends, Chidanand Saraswati, put it, "What else can we do? God is so great, She provides everything for us. God is the light. All we can do is offer our little lights to the great Light. We can only express our gratitude."

The question of one God versus many gods confounds every westerner who approaches Hinduism. On the apparent level, Hinduism has many gods who are depicted by *murtis*, statues or idols. Idolatry, of course, is not only condemned in the Biblical second commandment, it even contradicts the much less doctrinaire seven Noahide commandments that are said to be obligatory for all descendants of Noah, which is to say everyone.

Yet when the swami speaks of God as the Light, beyond all form and distinctions, this apparent level of understanding is put into question. And the more one delves into the philosophies underlying Hindu practice, the more the apparent level is exposed as a mere comic book version of a profound and serious theology. At the same time, some of the practices of Hinduism cannot be affirmed from a Jewish standpoint.

Yet, yet, yet. Something of any religious tradition is embodied in cultured persons raised in that tradition's more refined, philosophic threads. A Muslim who knows Islam's traditions, who earnestly strives to live up to the Qur'an's teachings and the exemplary life of its Prophet, is an impressive individual. The elegant courtesy of a Confucian gentleman who has improved his character by years of study and moral impeccability tells me more about Confucianism than any number of books and histories.

In just the same way, a cultured Hindu inspires everyone, Hindu and non-Hindu alike. His affectionate acceptance of all faiths, his soft-spoken gentleness, his kindness to all life whether human or animal—these are formidable virtues. Some years ago, my wife and I were visiting Benares. I wanted to show her a place where I had resided in the early 1970s, when I was studying Sanskrit and Indian philosophy at Benares Hindu University.

One of the professors at BHU with whom I retained a strong friendship kindly invited us for dinner. L. N. Sharma, a scholar of the Shaiva traditions of Kashmir, is a traditional Brahmin as well as a modern critical scholar. The BHU campus is a long way from the city, so he recommended that we hire a rickshaw and have the driver wait while we spent the evening with his family, because it might not be easy to find a rickshaw for the return journey. We had a tasty vegetarian meal and a delightful conversation. But what struck both of us was how Professor Sharma treated the rickshaw driver. One might expect a Brahmin to hardly even notice a rickshawallah, likely a low-caste person. Because it was so at variance with what we thought we knew of Indian society, and perhaps because the professor's actions were so exceptional, the kindness with which Professor Sharma brought out dinner for the rickshawallah was striking. Speaking softly and most courteously, the professor looked after the rickshawallah, making sure he had enough food and was comfortable. When the professor treated the menial driver as a guest, I knew beyond any doubt that Hinduism teaches *derekh eretz*, a way of being in the world that is consonant with the Jewish principle that all humans are created in the image of God (*be-tzelem E-lokim*). Whatever we may think of its more mundane religious practices, it cannot be denied that Hinduism creates a cultured human whose actions honor both humans and our Creator.

A Seminar at BHU

Professor Sharma's predecessor as head of BHU's department of philosophy was T. R. V. Murti, one of the most highly regarded academic philosophers of twentieth-century India. Like Professor Sharma, Professor Murti was a cultured Brahmin, a human of vast heart complemented by forceful intellect. Professor Murti was also the dissertation director for Professor Bibhuti S. Yadav, who was my dissertation director at Temple University. So according to both Hindu and academic tradition, Professor Murti was my grandfather.

Murti's scholarship concentrated on India's non-dual tradition known as Advaita Vedanta. Advaita is a thread within the esoteric textual tradition known as Vedanta, based on the *Upanishads*, some of the most elevated and inspiring works of literature in human history. As an incredulous French coal miner said to Larry Durrell in W. Somerset Maugham's *The Razor's Edge*, a favorite novel of mine, "What? You say you have never read the *Upanishads*? And you call yourself educated?" I agree with this sentiment entirely, and I repeat it to my students more often than they care to hear. One simply isn't well read unless one has seriously studied this masterpiece.

Advaita is codified in the writings of the eighth-century philosopher-saint Shankara, arguably the greatest Indian thinker of all time. It is a strict monism, or non-dualism. The universal essence known as Brahman is identical to the essence of the individual, or Atman. "That are Thou" is the dictum of the *Upanishads*, which teach that the everyday experience of duality is our own imposition on Reality, a limitation of the infinite, a magical display known as *Maya*. "Truth is at the back of things," say the sages, and meditation when coupled with a life of study and virtuous conduct can lead one to the transformative experience of Oneness. This experience is known as liberation (*moksha*) or enlightenment (*nirvana*).

To read Shankara's texts with a master is to bathe oneself in the purest mystical philosophy; it is inspiring, elegant, beautiful not only for the language and ideas themselves, but also for where those words and thoughts transport the student. To have read these jewels with Professor Murti is one of the great intellectual intoxications of my life. It was intellectual because of Shankara's precise and irrefutable logic, and it was intoxicating because following that logic leads one to see through Maya's veils and confront Reality with a scintillating clarity.

It really wasn't so surprising, then, that a foreign Christian student at BHU was carried away. He came to Murti with great emotion, the story goes, and told his teacher that he was so taken with Advaita that he wanted to convert to Hinduism to follow it as his life's mission.

It was the only time this student, or any of Murti's students, had seen the professor become angry. "If you think you should convert to Hinduism," he told him, "then you have utterly misunderstood everything I have been trying to teach. You insult both Hinduism and your own Christianity." With an angry gesture, he dismissed the crestfallen student and never spoke to him again.

I sympathize with both the student and the professor. The student fully expected to be embraced into Hinduism just as someone born Hindu might be welcomed should he decide to become Christian. This view is part-and-parcel of the Christian student's religious worldview. But just as foundationally, the professor understood Advaita as a way of understanding a religion and not as a religion in itself. Therefore, he would believe, a Christian who appreciates non-dualism should bring that understanding to his own Christianity.[2]

For traditional Hindu and Buddhist teachers, religion is not a banner or an allegiance. It is a way of improving people, of enhancing compassion and wisdom. To switch religions is impossible because one is born into a society and a family for important reasons, and the anguish a conversion would cause

---

[2] I was told this story by Prof. Harold C. Coward.

to one's own community is utterly, thoroughly unjustifiable and ultimately selfish.

In this spirit, the fourth-century Hindu lawgiver, Manu, wrote that to look after another person's religion is a sin akin to adultery, of lusting after something that is not properly one's own. Therefore, Manu concluded, the wise king must outlaw conversion as a prerequisite for social and familial harmony.

Manu's view is also rooted in the unshakeable Hindu conviction that all religions are paths leading to the same goal. Metaphors abound to make this point, but it is a cultural bedrock assumption in India, and it gently challenges an equally bedrock assumption in most of the western world, that religions are by nature competitive and truth resides in one but not all. Many westerners celebrate conversions as triumphs, the family heartbreak and the disruption to society be damned.

Lamps, Light, and Festivals

Traditional Hindus and Jews live in a lunar-calendric universe, at least some of the time. Unlike Muslims, who disdain intercalation (adjusting a lunar calendar to the solar-driven seasons), Jews and Hindus adapt their calendars to ancient agricultural needs. Therefore, the celebrations of the Hindu festival Holi and the Jewish festival Purim often fall during the same springtime full moon. Likewise, Hanukkah follows Diwali by as little as half a lunar cycle—when it isn't a leap year. Tantalizingly, these two pairs of festivals bear strong affinities: Holi and Purim are times for inebriated merrymaking. And Diwali and Hanukkah are both known as "the festival of light," and kindling lamps plays a major role in both.

My most recent visit to Benares, in 2004, coincided with Diwali. After sundown the *ghats* became even more magical than usual. Here in the city of Shiva, people worship Mother River, blending devotional hymns to Vishnu's incarnations with paeans to Shiva. Such embodied ecumenism is woven into the social fabric of Benares. It must be no coincidence, then, that weaving has been the Muslims' chief craft in this area for a thousand years.

Aarti—worship that includes waving a lighted lamp to the Mother River—commenced as a huge red moon rose above the horizon. Spirited devotional songs (*bhajans*) accompanied the graceful *aarti* offering of lamps. By the time the moon hung above the River, the *bhajans* were replaced by a concert of classical vocal music. Blazing wicks on folded leaves floated by. Devotees constantly rang bells to hail the God or gods nearby. It was the kind of spiritual and aesthetic beauty I have found only in India, and I felt a deep satisfaction as I drank in the ambience.

Jerusalem and Benares

In the audience, Israeli youth seemed to outnumber all the Europeans and Americans combined. Hebrew was as frequent in my ears as it had been in my eyes as I read notices about *kriya yoga* classes or a falafel restaurant posted along the *ghats*. And my new, younger colleagues at BHU were abuzz about the university's recently signed linkage with Hebrew University, as fitting an academic partnership as could be found anywhere.

Jerusalem and Benares. These two cities could be joined with one another in one sentence because there is no city anywhere that compares with either. Each city has borne a continuous culture for more than three thousand years. They each have a palpable spiritual presence that draws pilgrims and tourists like iron filings to a magnet.

And each is the focus of followers of offshoot religions, Buddhism and Christianity. Lord Buddha preached his first sermon at nearby Sarnath, where Buddhist pilgrims from Japan, Thailand, Sri Lanka, and the west pay their respects, just as Christians and Muslims have special relationships with Jerusalem, particularly the former. I chuckled to see a ritual rivalry between Thai and Tibetan Buddhists as each group circumambulated the huge *stupa* (a bell-shaped reliquary) erected by the third-century B.C.E. Emperor Ashoka, one of history's most enlightened rulers and even today a model for a religiously pluralistic national polity. The Thai group, led by saffron-robed monks, chanted in Pali, while the Tibetan lamas, in maroon robes, led their western students in chanting mantras and performing worship. It reminded me so much of a visit to Jerusalem's Church of the Holy Sepulchre, where Jesus is said to have been crucified, buried, and resurrected. A group of foreign Roman Catholics said their Mass at Golgotha, and it seemed as if the Greek Orthodox priests couldn't wait for them to finish so they could wave their own incense to cover the offending aroma of the Roman offering.

Most of us think of Judaism, Christianity, and Islam as the three western monotheisms, as though monotheism never existed in India. Some politely refer to them as the three Abrahamic faiths, as Abraham is taken to be their father, either in a literal or a spiritualized sense. These western religions are assumed to be distinct from "eastern religions," which are characterized by a cyclic view of history and multiple deities. Indeed, that is one way to make a general distinction.

But it is not the only way, as I tell my students. The western/eastern distinction conceals as much as it reveals, and when one's attention is focused on Judaism and Hinduism, another new model presents itself: the old/new distinction. The world's ancient religions—Judaism, Hinduism, and the Chinese tradition we have come to call Confucianism—share more than a history of some four thousand years. These ancient faiths address all aspects of life from ethics to law, medicine, art, politics, literature, social theory, astrology, and the performing arts. They fill all these roles because in ancient times knowledge had not yet been fragmented into discrete fields. Knowledge was religion, religion was knowledge.

The newer religions—Buddhism, Christianity, and Islam—could focus their interests. The first two, the original offspring, developed around a charismatic leader who accepted the basic worldview of the parent faith, but chose to focus on spirituality. Just as Jesus was born, lived, taught, and died as a Jew, so, too, the Buddha was born, lived, taught, and died as a Hindu. Christianity, for example, simply accepted the Judaic worldview of creation and went on from there. The Buddha's famous lack of cosmological interest was due to the absence of any need to develop a cosmology of his own; he simply assumed Hindu accounts of creation. In both cases, for reasons more cultural or political than religious, followers of the Buddha and of the Christ ended up creating new religions named for their renegade founders.

Islam is something of a special case, because it in many ways tried to restore Judaism's social ethos, rejecting Christianity's spiritualized otherworldliness, while at the same time retaining Christianity's "universalism" or missionary zeal. This old/new paradigm opens up new perspectives on other features of the two types of faiths, including the tendency for old religions to remain wedded to a land and/or a people, whereas the new faiths seek to spread their convictions through empires. Christianity became insignificant in Israel, just as Buddhism all but vanished from India. Each found more fertile soils outside their motherlands. On another track, the new religions had to articulate reasons why the old ones were unsatisfactory, resulting in some pretty unkind views of their parents. I could go on and on (as my students might attest), but the central point is that when our examples are Judaism and Hinduism, we generalize different facets of religion than when our data are rooted in Christian categories.

The juxtaposition of Jerusalem and Benares invites such speculations. And now, though it is long overdue, generally unimaginative academic administrators and bureaucrats have acknowledged the deep cultural resonance between them. Benares Hindu University, the largest residential university in all of Asia, and the Hebrew University of Jerusalem, a bastion of secularism in one of the world's most holy cities, have discovered one another.

7

A Concentration Camp in Tea Country
Sri Lanka

~

Upon learning that I am reasonably well traveled, acquaintances often ask what I consider to be the most beautiful place I have ever visited. I love the question, because it sends my mind back to some wonderful places indeed. Capri comes to mind, as does Alaska's Kenai Peninsula. And there is the view of massive Annapurna from the trekking trails near Pokhara in Nepal, as well as Makenna beach in Maui. Recalling such places is akin to counting one's blessings. For a kid from Camden, it is heady even to imagine such beauty.

But when I come out of my reveries of volcanic Pacific beaches, Himalayan mountains, and Italian gardens, I find myself describing Sri Lanka. As gorgeous as the east coast resorts of Batticaloa and Trincomalee are, as inspiring as the Dambulla cave temples are, or the sacred complex of Kataragama, as wild as Yala National Park is, as sublime as the sunsets framed by swaying palm trees near Galle can be, it is in the tea-growing hill country in the central part of the island where my soul merges with nature. There, my mind seems no longer limited by my body as it travels from waterfall to ridge to verdant tea plantation, all appearing within arm's reach from my vantage point atop a hill. Extravagant flora bloom precariously on the steep mountainsides, while tropical birds soar, and variety after variety of monkeys swing through the trees. So fertile is the blessed island that you can literally hear bamboo growing if you remain still enough. The brilliant green color of young rice in the checkerboard rice paddies nestled on mountainsides rushes along the optic nerve into the brain and refreshes the spirit just as spring reinvigorates the passions.

But the first time I went to Sri Lanka, I went for scholarship, not for scenery. I was off to learn Pali and read Buddhist scriptures.

An Interlude in Israel

After completing my doctoral coursework and comprehensive examinations in Philadelphia in 1976, I was extremely fortunate to win a Fulbright fellowship for dissertation research in Sri Lanka. With misgivings, I decided to stop in Israel en route. I had never been there, and my motivation was quite frankly my sense of obligation as a budding scholar of comparative religions. A visit to Jerusalem seemed to be a prerequisite for my professional life.

If that sounds diffident, I was. I am not at all proud of the fact that at the time my opinion of Israel—and of Judaism—was mostly negative. Like so many of the "enlightened" people in American universities, I saw Israel as a colonial outpost in the Third World, the oppressor of another people. Similarly, despite my regard for Hasidism as conveyed by Martin Buber, and despite some nostalgia for the synagogues of my youth, I found Judaism rather dreary, especially compared with the elegant, direct spiritual teachings of eastern religions.

Some fellow graduate students recommended that I stay at a Franciscan pilgrims hospice in the Old City. From the United States, I posted my request for a room at that venerable establishment in an envelope addressed to the Franciscans in "Jerusalem, Occupied Territories, via Israel." As I write these words today, sitting in my comfortable office at the Shalom Hartman Institute in Jerusalem anticipating going to the Kotel (*ha-Kotel ha-Ma'aravi*, "Western Wall") to welcome the Sabbath this evening, I cringe at my words. But that is who I was.

I wish I could tell you that as soon as I set foot on Israel's holy soil, my heart melted and I made a profound *teshuvah* (return or repentance), but that isn't what happened. I felt more alienated than ever, but my feet seemed to find their own way to the Kotel. No matter where I intended to walk, somehow all paths led there, and indeed the very sight of this remnant of the Holy Temple inspired awe.

I was not even aware that this was during the autumn festival of Sukkot. During *hol ha-moed*, the intermediate days of the festival, I was walking aimlessly around the Old City. An Orthodox Jew saw me in my hippie–graduate student garb, and asked whether I was a *kohen* (hereditary priest). What I am about to write rekindles deep, heartfelt embarrassment. I did not know that on these intermediate days, it is considered especially auspicious to receive the Biblical threefold priestly benediction from a *kohen*. I said I was one, befuddled by what he had seen that provoked him to ask the question. He removed his cap, pointed to his *kippah*-clad head, and asked me to give him the bless-ing. I did not even know at the time what the blessing was! So I smiled and mumbled as if I knew. I have since learned that when delivering the benedic-tion, the priest is obligated to pronounce each word loud and distinctly, so he must have known I was faking. But he was gracious and good-natured enough to smile and thank me anyway before going on his way.

During that visit to Israel, I took tours with Christian Palestinian guides to the Church of the Holy Sepulchre and Gethsemane, to the Dome of the Rock, and also to Joseph's Tomb and Nazareth. I felt embarrassed by my very existence, for I was deeply experiencing the profound ambivalence that many Jews feel about our heritage. After my short and awkward visit, I was rather re-lieved to board an El Al plane to Teheran to escape my Jewish destiny . . . for just a while longer.

My Academic Game Plan

Having worked on Sanskrit and Tibetan in India and in the United States, I felt the need, in order to round out my understanding of Buddhism, to learn about the Theravada tradition as it is presented in its Pali texts and embodied in culture. Buddhists around the world see Sri Lanka as the home of the "purest" threads within the tradition. Even the rival Mahayana school affirms the legend of the Buddha's three visits to Lanka—as told in the *Lankavatara Sutra*—and his prophecy that his Dharma (teaching) would be uniquely pre-served on this "resplendent isle." Other Theravada societies—Burma, Thai-land, Kampuchea, and Laos—affirm Sri Lanka's religious preeminence and priority, so this was the place for me. My plan was to spend a year, which turned out to be closer to two, learning Pali, essentially a Sanskrit dialect in which the Theravada sacred corpus is preserved, and reading through the en-tire collection of the Buddha's discourses (*suttas*, or *sutras* in Sanskrit), which are the heart of the canon.

My choice of a dissertation topic was informed by sensitivities inculcated by my Jewish background, although I did not come to realize that until years later. I grew up in a world where my people's sacred book was considered to be an "old" testament, at best a preparation for a "new" one that replaced, ful-filled, or abrogated it, depending on which Christian theological strand one adopts. For the Jew, of course, the Hebrew Bible is sufficient, the covenant made between God and Abraham and refined at Sinai is eternal, and whatever validity Christianity may or may not have has no impact on God's loving re-lationship with the Jewish people.

Coming from such a background, I bristled at some of the claims in Mahayana Buddhist texts that earlier Buddhist schools were really "inferior vehicles" (the real meaning of *hinayana*, a pejorative term), or that the "worthy
saints" (*arahants* or, in Sanskrit, *arhats*) among the Buddha's disciples were
not truly enlightened but were arrogantly deluded in believing they had attained *nirvana* (*nibbana* in Pali).

Knowing (or believing) that Judaism was a direct path to God that left its
followers with no need to seek "fulfillment" elsewhere, I instinctively felt that
there was a similar truth to be brought to the study of Buddhism: that the
Theravada was as much a path to enlightenment as the Mahayana. So I decided to focus my dissertation on the descriptions of the ideal person in three
Buddhist traditions: the worthy *arahant* of the Theravada, the compassionate
bodhisattva of the Mahayana, and the magical *mahasiddha* of the Vajrayana. By
delving into texts (in Pali, Sanskrit, and Tibetan, respectively), while privately
practicing the meditations of each school, I hoped to come to an understanding of how these three images could be harmonized and reconciled. My am-
bitious hope was that I could demonstrate my findings based on textual
sources, and then generalize a theoretical approach to the question of how to
interpret the derogatory claims made by a "new" religion about the "older" religion from which it had emerged. If I could analyze this phenomenon using
intra-Buddhist disputations as my data, then perhaps my methodology could
be applied to the strained relationship between Christianity and Judaism. Of
course, at the time I did not know that this was my personal agenda, and that
I was really working through issues from my own childhood and from the experiences of my beleaguered, demeaned people.

Trouble in Paradise

Upon arrival in Sri Lanka in the late summer of 1976, I headed up-country to Kandy, medieval capital and bastion of Singhalese culture, once the last
holdout against the juggernaut of the British Empire. The Kandyan kings
valiantly resisted the British, who had replaced the Dutch overlords of the lit-
toral coast, who in turn had replaced the Portuguese. But the kings could re-
sist only so long, and in 1848 ceded sovereignty to London, whose
Queen-Empress Victoria assumed the Kandyan kings' royal obligation as de-
fender of the faith of Buddhism. Apparently the British had no sense of irony
about their contradictory roles.

In Sri Lanka, I came to learn about an eccentric American named Colonel
Henry Steele Olcott, a minor hero of the Civil War who incidentally had

chaired the commission that investigated Lincoln's assassination. The colonel, following the distinctly American tradition of the Transcendentalists, became enamored of eastern spirituality, and sailed to Galle around 1880 on his quest for enlightenment. Somewhere along the way he became associated with Madame Blavatsky and Annie Besant, and the three became leaders of the Theosophical Society. Olcott found that Ceylon, as the British renamed the island, was a subjugated culture. Far from defending Buddhism, British colonial rulers had dismantled its role in society, and in education in particular. Christian missionary schools flourished, but by the late nineteenth century not one Buddhist college remained.

Deferring his own spiritual quest, the colonel embarked with typically American activism on a project to resurrect a moribund Buddhism. He traveled throughout the country in a bullock cart, giving fiery speeches and raising funds, penny by penny, to establish Buddhist schools to rival the missionaries' institutions. And he did so, founding two fine colleges. His combative spirit let him into disputations with missionaries. He pamphleteerd and cajoled his way to becoming a national hero of sorts. Even today, his statue, replete with a long beard, stands outside the Colombo railway station, the only foreigner so honored in this nationalistic country.

My own impatience with missionaries and defense of the Theravada against Mahayana invectives led a number of my colleagues and acquaintances to identify me with the colonel. My hirsute visage probably made this identification all the easier, and I was frankly flattered by the comparison.

Although I quickly became enamored of lovely Kandy and impressed with the faculty at the university in nearby Peradeniya, I was not able to remain. As so often happens, student unrest over the issue de jour made the campus dangerous, at least in the minds of the embassy officials who bore responsibility for my well-being. With reluctance, I settled into life in Colombo, the westernized coastal capital, and resumed my research at Vidyalanaka University in nearby Kelaniya. I jumped into studying Pali and reading the sacred texts. What I did not realize at the time, of course, was that the minor flare-up on the Peradeniya campus was but a prelude to what was to come in the months and decades to follow.

With Monks and Nuns

Perhaps the most rewarding aspect of my years in Sri Lanka was the people I came to know. I think that people from smaller countries are, of necessity, more cosmopolitan, more open to the larger world, than people from massive nations who can somehow afford the delusion that meaningful life ends at their borders. Americans, Indians, and Chinese tend to suffer this type of xenophobia, while Sri Lankans are the opposite. Many go abroad for their advanced degrees. The news media in Sri Lanka, whether in English or a vernacular, brim with news from abroad. Foreign films, novels, and music are the stuff of dinner table conversation. The very smallness of such countries carries with it a negation of excessive self-importance.

One of the remarkable people I came to know was a scholar regarded as among the very most erudite monks not only on the island, but also in the entire Theravada world. The late Venerable Nyanaponika Mahathera was a "monk's monk," someone to consult when you are confronted with a particularly thorny problem of exegesis of the sacred texts. He was one of the people I simply had to meet.

When the inevitable happened, when I could not understand how to read a *shloka* (verse) in a text and could get no satisfactory explanation from my university colleagues, I journeyed up to Kandy to meet the senior monk. He lived in a small hut known as the "Forest Hermitage," located above the town in the middle of a wildlife preserve. As I approached the hut, I saw him—a pale, slight man who was busily feeding, and seemingly conversing with, a horde of monkeys. It crossed my mind that there was something Saint Francis–like about their interactions. Catching my breath in such a presence, I approached and was warmly greeted with a strong, sweet cup of fine tea.

He was able to resolve my textual conundrum easily, and we chatted. What I had not anticipated was that this eminent Buddhist monk was a German Jew. He had fled the rise of Nazism in his homeland and, already having an abiding interest in Buddhism, made his way to India to seek a refuge, refuge from Hitler and refuge in the Triple Gem of Buddhism. He got both.

I learned that he and a number of other like-minded German Jews shared a similar story. Settling in India, they found their spiritual quest interrupted by the wartime security concerns of the British Raj. To the British, they were German nationals and, as such, "enemy aliens" who posed a threat. Ignoring the obvious fact that they were Jews, the British interned them for the duration of the war. A number ended up in Dehra Dun, a charming North Indian hill station, where, as Nyanaponika put it, they turned their prison into an ashram. They meditated. They debated controversies between Hinduism and Buddhism, and between the rival Mahayana and Theravada in particular. Nyanaponika's favorite interlocutor was to become known as the Lama Anagarika Govinda, an esteemed author and lay teacher of the Tibetan Mahayana.

These early "HinJews" and "JuBus" included spiritual seekers, religious leaders, and academics—all part of an unlikely and unknown footnote to the history of the Holocaust.

Another such personality was the late Ayyah (Sister) Khema, who was admired both as a meditation teacher and as an activist on behalf of Buddhist women.

Ever since the time of the Buddha, monks and nuns have spent the three-month monsoon season in retreat, practicing intensive meditation, studying sacred texts, and perhaps composing edifying treatises to benefit fellow seekers. During one such retreat, I first met Ayyah Khema.

Among the most highly regarded Buddhist nuns in the world, she headed a Buddhist temple in Australia, and had constructed a women's meditation and retreat center on a remote island in Sri Lanka. She regularly taught meditation on five continents, and Buddhists around the world sought her sage counsel. In fact, visiting Buddhist laywomen, offering alms and requesting a sympathetic ear, frequently interrupted her retreat.

Certainly, none of them knew that Ayyah Khema was a Jew. Born in pre-war Berlin into an upper-class, highly assimilated Jewish family, she attended the best schools and avidly enjoyed German culture. She grew up with servants and soirées, music and poetry, but very little Jewishness.

Her father had the perspicacity to get his family out of Germany while it was still possible. They found their way to Shanghai, where they waited out Germany's madness, and where he continued his business amid a cosmopolitan Jewish community. Here Ayyah Khema first encountered Jewish mysticism.

One war followed another. Mao's revolution forced the family out of China, and they made their circuitous way to California, where she eventually married and raised children and grandchildren.

Whether from innate inclination or because of her remarkable experiences, Ayyah Khema's interest in mysticism grew. Having read Gershom Scholem's studies of Kabbalah, she wrote to him in Jerusalem, asking for advice about to how to begin studying Kabbalah experientially.

She later understood how naive her letter was. Some months later, she received a curt reply. "He told me to forget about it, that a woman—especially one who lacked an extensive background in Torah and Talmud—was prohibited from ever approaching these mystical treasures of Jewish tradition," she remembered. "So I continued to read and study on my own."

Her eclectic readings included spiritual masterpieces from the east. She was especially impressed with Buddhist literature. Its directness, its freedom from metaphysical and ritual embellishment, was naturally attractive, especially considering her frustration at the traditional barriers safeguarding Jewish mysticism. The openness of Buddhist teachers proved even more important than her theoretical concerns. One did not have to be of a certain age or ethnicity, or gender, or especially learned or observant, as a prerequisite for learning mystical practices. At least, this is true of the Buddhism that is exported to the west. Ayyah Khema jumped at the opportunity.

Her study of Buddhism and practice of meditation grew, and after the death of her husband, she took ordination as a Buddhist nun. "Of course I'm still Jewish. What else could I be?" she replied to my unasked question. "Jewish is something you *are*, and I am proud of our heritage." Our conversation was punctuated with words from both Yiddish and Pali. Her manner was suffused with Buddhist compassion and Jewish warmth.

I reflected that it was too bad she had not been born twenty years later, at a time when women could approach Kabbalah without quite so many barriers. How much contemporary Judaism needs powerful, spiritual, female teachers! I felt that the loss was Judaism's, not Ayyah Khema's, since it was evident that her life was so very rich, that her spirit had grown so strong.

Ayyah Khema's eclectic spiritual path is a precursor to contemporary trends in Jewish women's spirituality. Two factors, one on the right and one on the left, have opened the tradition's spiritual treasures to women. For one thing, knowledge of the Hebrew language, once the exclusive domain of men in *yeshivot*, has become much more widespread, due in part to study programs in Israel. There is no substitute for working with texts in the original languages, and Hebrew is the key to unlock them. Spending a post–high school year learning in seminaries in Israel, a common practice among the Orthodox, has enabled women to continue to study and to learn at unprecedented levels. On the other side, liberal Judaism has internalized the larger society's views on gender equality, and now women routinely become Reform, Conservative, Reconstructionist, or Renewal rabbis, and their training is often overlaid upon experience with eastern meditation. The result is the palpable presence of female spiritual teachers around the Jewish world today. Highly encouraging trends, in my opinion, much overdue, and in some cases too late.

An Elephant Never Forgets

For a while, I feared that I might be developing paranoia. Running errands here and there around Colombo on my motorcycle, it seemed that over and over again, I saw an odd-looking short man eyeing me in a strange way.

He seemed to be almost everywhere, and his attention was always focused on me. On day I drove up to the office of the United States Educational Foundation to pick up my mail. The office was on a side street, so I was especially disconcerted to find him there, waiting for me, as it were. As I dismounted my motorcycle, I saw him hold his hands before his eyes, making a kind of box frame by jutting out his thumbs at right angles to his fingers. Before I could do anything, he approached me.

"Have you ever done any acting?" he said in lieu of a greeting. I surprised myself by answering him directly, saying that I had while in college. In fact, I loved the stage, a dalliance that has proven to be of inestimable value in developing my pedagogic and lecturing skills.

"You are perfect," he continued. "I want you in my new film."

I felt like Lana Turner at the Schwab's drug store soda fountain! Was I being discovered? It turned out that this odd-looking fellow was ever odder than I could have guessed. He was Manik Sandrasagra, *enfant terrible* of Colombo society, a provocative, brilliant Tamil filmmaker known for his mystical iconoclasm, multifarious entrepreneurial projects, advocacy of marijuana legalization, and generally scandalous life. Over cups of tea, he told me about himself and his new film, about his devotion to Lord Shiva, and about the corruption of Sri Lanka's indigenous culture. He claimed to have been both a junior writer for the 1960s-era Smothers Brothers television program and a salesman for Israel Bonds in Canada. I have been unable to verify either of these claims.

Well, who wouldn't want to be in a film, at least once in a lifetime? So I agreed to play a supporting role as an animal-loving, mildly mystical Anglican priest who lived in the up-country tea-growing area. The film was to star Sri Lanka's top leading man, Gamini Fonseka, and Mary Tamm, a little-known Hollywood actress. The film was entitled *Rampage*, pronounced in the Singhalese style as *Ram-pa-gay*. It was actually shown at Cannes, and I even received complimentary reviews on my acting. Thenceforth, it seemed as if filmmakers invited me to play the role of the foreigner in every movie made in the country for the next year or so, but once was enough for me. Besides, I had a dissertation to write.

Rampage was about a tea planter (Fonseka) who hunted big game and British women with equal skill. Yet he retained an intimate relationship with his priest (me), engaging in mystical theological discussions over a round of golf. It seems that this planter once shot a female elephant, whose calf witnessed the horrifying murder. The calf grew up and, of course, planned revenge against his mother's killer. The now-adult elephant goes on a rampage, and the priest counsels the planter to forsake hunting because "all creatures are, first and foremost, an idea in the mind of God" and therefore sacred. The film ends with the planter impaled on the elephant's tusks.

I found film acting to be extremely difficult, tiring work. Unlike stage acting, which takes place in real time, film acting involves, more than anything else, waiting around for the technical crew to get the set ready, all the while remaining in character. I found such sustained concentration draining, but it was an experience not to be missed.

Sometimes the delays in filming were for more exotic reasons than a glitch in the lighting. Once, shooting was postponed for several days because the lead elephant caught a cold. The attentive *mahout* (elephant trainer) explained the treatment. "First, you buy five loaves of white bread and six bottles of rum," he told me. "You cut the loaves lengthwise, soak the bread with five of the bottles of rum and feed them to the elephant. After about three days of sleep, the elephant will be fit again." And the sixth bottle of rum? "Oh, since the elephant won't be working for a few days, I drink that one myself!"

The best part of working on the film, however, was entering Manik's world—a mix of Colombo society and the rural Hindu mystics found more frequently around Sri Lanka than one would imagine. Manik introduced me to Supreme Court justices, business magnates, rural activists attempting to resurrect an "authentic" indigenous agrarian culture, and a plethora of artists and writers.

We did much of the filming in Nuwara Eliya, the highest of the British-era hill stations, at more than seven thousand feet in elevation above even the verdant tea plantations that dominate much of the up-country. The cast and crew were put up at the Grand Hotel, which probably had been just *that* at one time. After long days on the set, we welcomed even the rotgut local whiskey. As we drank and smoked, tales of the British "good old days" permeated the oak-paneled lounge.

On one such evening, word reached us that the island had become convulsed in a spasm of violence between the ethnic majority Singhalese, most of whom are Buddhists but a significant number of whom are Christians, and the minority Tamils, mostly Hindu, but with an even larger Christian minority. The island's Muslims were ambiguously placed between the rival camps, although they were Tamil speakers who identified more with the Singhalese.

The area in and around Nuwara Eliya was especially hard hit by the violence, and as soon as the government lifted the round-the-clock curfew for a few hours, we headed back to Colombo as quickly as we could. As we drove, we saw burned-out shops and an occasional mutilated corpse by the side of the road.

The violence shocked me, although longtime observers of Sri Lanka were more sanguine. They recalled the 1971 "insurrection" led by an ultra-left, Khmer Rouge–like faction known as the Janatha Vimukthi Perumatha, or JVP. The bloody turmoil came within a hair's breadth of toppling the government, and periodic outbursts of communal violence became the rule of the land.

I recall a discussion I had about this with the Cornell linguist Jim Gair, America's leading Sinhala (the language of the Singhalese) scholar, who was also there on a Fulbright grant. I told him that I couldn't imagine how such a seemingly gentle, soft-spoken people with a culture based on a pacific religion like Buddhism could indulge in the sort of brutality we had just witnessed. Over his commissary-bought Johnny Walker, Gair scoffed at my naiveté. It is just a mask, he said, a veneer of gentility. Beneath the surface lay bloody passions; the more gentle people appear, he concluded, the more violent is their underbelly. His neo-Freudian analysis perplexed me, but how could I argue with someone who had spent years in a country where I was so new?

As future visits to Sri Lanka were to make clear, Jim's analysis was not far off the mark.

In a Concentration Camp

Another of my favorite Sri Lankans is something of an ongoing scandal in the Buddhist Studies world. Philosophy professor Gunapala Dharmasiri is, frankly, more interested in evenings of classical Indian music, his delightful family, and his work in support of educational opportunities for Sri Lanka's Buddhist nuns than in writing learned articles or guiding doctoral dissertations. He is also passionate about Jews and Israel.

He often teaches American students who come to the island on one or another study-abroad program, and many of those students are Jewish. He manages to identify and befriend them, inspiring them to take another, deeper look at their own culture and religion. He admires the Jewish intellectual heritage, and likes to say, "With Jewish intelligence and Buddhist patience, there is nothing that cannot be accomplished."

He is on to something there. Cultivation of the intellect, a life of study, is nowhere so highly valued as in Jewish culture. In no other universe could an extravaganza like the celebration of the completion of the seven-and-a-half year cyclic study of the Talmud, the 2005 *Siyum ha-Shas*, captivate an entire people in an unparalleled celebration of learning.

Complementarily, patience is a cardinal virtue in the Buddhist world, but it is not very highly esteemed elsewhere—perhaps especially not in Judaism. It takes time for the profundity of patience to sink into a Jewish mind, and Dharmasiri's adage is a useful pointer. The Dalai Lama forcefully makes the same point when he comments about the Chinese occupiers of his beloved Tibet. He teaches that one must be grateful to one's enemy above all, because an enemy can teach us something that no one else can: patience.

Intellect and patience. The possibilities of their conjunction are staggering.

Acerbic as always, Dharmasiri poked fun at the western world's fascination with meditation. Sri Lanka's meditation centers rightly are well regarded throughout the world, and many westerners come to the island expressly to learn the ancient techniques. Dharmasiri scoffs good-naturedly: "These foreigners always want to come to our concentration camps. Now why would a Jew go to so much trouble just to sit in a concentration camp?" Such diffidence notwithstanding, I found a "mindfulness" course of inestimable value to my own development. I did one at Nilambé, which perches up a steep, switchback-filled dusty trail above Peradeniya, and is generally considered one of the most serious meditation centers in the Buddhist world. I settled into my room, a cell actually, with trepidation at the thought of so much silence, so much intensive self-scrutiny. And it is not that these reservations ever left, but that I came to accept them. And that may be the key to understanding what this technique is all about.

The Buddha learned meditation from his Hindu teachers, and he acknowledged the value and efficacy of what he had learned. Meditation calms the mind, and bestows a sense of peace and well-being. Today we might say it is a stress-buster that lowers the blood pressure. All of that is true.

The meditations that the Buddha learned are known as "trance"—*jhana* in Pali or *dhyana* in Sanskrit. When Buddhism was introduced into China, *dhyana* was pronounced as *ch'an*, and when it moved to Korea the name was said as *son*, and finally in Japan it became known as *zen*. This technique is said to lead to supernormal powers, some unrelated to spiritual growth or self-understanding, such as the ability to fly or walk on water; but others, such as the ability to read minds, to know other people's karmic propensities and destinies, and even to remember one's past lives, were considered valuable as a pedagogic tools, even if not as a requisite for enlightenment. This is what the Buddha affirmed from Hindu teachings.

But he also separated himself from the tradition of his birth, and he taught forms of meditation of his own creation, and these are known as *vipassana* (insight) or *sati* (mindfulness) meditations. These techniques, he taught, led to a distinctively Buddhist goal, *nibbana* in Pali or *nirvana* in Sanskrit. What is taught in the Theravada world today is actually a combination of the two, using trance meditation as a warm-up, yielding the calmness deemed essential for deeper self-exploration and culminating in the development of insight.

The practice begins with a resolution to sit still and concentrate on one's out-breath for a fixed, relatively short period of time. Of course, this sounds much easier than it is, because someone who is not trained in meditation will find even ten minutes of stillness too much to bear. During a meditation retreat, one spends around ten hours a day practicing. Very soon after one begins sitting, bodily aches and pains abound. Itches become maddening. Mosquitoes are like tormentors from hell. And this is before thoughts even arise, and then it becomes far more difficult to let thoughts be. The point is that we normally react to stimuli with no pause. We feel an itch so we scratch. We hear a buzz so we swat. Meditation demands that we neither scratch nor swat, but that we just sit. The backaches become excruciating, the buzzes deafening. But we sit for as long as we can, as still as we can. It takes will to return, again and again, to the ever-present out-breath. After some practice, we can do it for a few minutes, and the ache dissipates, the buzz ceases to be annoying.

Actually, mosquitoes play a role in the life of a Theravada meditator. In diaries kept by medieval Sri Lankan "forest-dwelling" monks, mosquitoes figure prominently. Rather than swat them or fear their bite, the meditator gradually becomes able to offer his or her blood as a gift of food to the mosquito, which also needs to eat and live. This is Buddhist patience. This is generosity. This is compassion. And this is utterly maddening to one who is not on their level!

But one makes progress, and the backaches lessen as one's concentration increases. And once these bodily issues recede, then one can watch thoughts rise, last, and fall with the same patient equanimity that one applies to aches and pains. And when one becomes a bit proficient in watching thoughts come and go, one learns to direct attention to painful memories and view them with the same patience, equanimity, and dispassion. One slowly becomes able to increase the pause or gap between stimulus and response, and the peace of mind that the Buddha proclaimed is to be found precisely there, in that pause.

These days, when I teach my students about Buddhism, I try to apply this type of meditation to contemporary life. What the mosquito was in medieval Sri Lanka, our freeways' worst drivers are to contemporary America. I have a rough commute from my Miami Beach home to my university, and the freeway's aggressive drivers are my mosquitoes. Now, when I am cut off, or slowed, or detoured, I strive to rediscover the gap between those stimuli and the resulting anger, my wish to retaliate in road rage. Of course, I still get angry, but I try very hard to watch that anger rise, last, and dissipate, rather than flip the adversarial driver a proverbial bird. Once in a while, it works. At least my students get the point of meditation more readily.

8

The Lama and the Rebbe
Boulder, Colorado

~

Returning to Philadelphia, I wrote my dissertation in 1978 and received an offer to teach Buddhist Studies at Naropa Institute (now Naropa University), a Buddhist college in Boulder, Colorado. But my route to Boulder meandered from Sri Lanka via the Bay of Bengal and through New York, so we have to back up just a bit.

One day early in 1973 I was swimming in the Bay of Bengal at Puri, a holy city in Orissa, when I quite literally bumped into another swimmer. When we reached the shore, we chatted and I learned that his name was Reggie Ray and he was completing his doctoral dissertation on Tantric Buddhism at the University of Chicago. Since I was just about to begin graduate studies, I was keenly interested in everything he had to tell me, and we became friends. He was a devotee of the Kagyupa sect of Tibetan Buddhism, and when he heard that I was then on my way to Sikkim to work at the Tibetology institute there, he told me I simply had to meet his guru's guru, the Gwalya Karmapa.

While studying in Sikkim a short time later, I visited him at his monastery at nearby Rumtek, and I felt a strong connection with the master. He seemed to be struck by my then red, flowing beard, and he dubbed me "the incomparable *rishi*," or seer. That fall, back in America, I learned that the Karmapa was coming to New York City to perform the esoteric Black Crown ceremony, his specialty. This was an event I simply could not miss.

When I went to New York for the ceremony in early 1974, I was introduced to the Karmapa's student and Reggie's teacher, the Venerable Chögyam Trungpa Rinpoche. Just by accident, as it were, I had the privilege of being present during some quiet time the guru spent with his disciple, and I keenly remember the highly charged, emotional encounter. For what seemed like a long time, the Karmapa, sitting regally on his Dharma throne, cradled Trungpa's head in his lap, gently stroking his hair as both men wept. The

Karmapa spoke softly into Trungpa's ear. I could only guess as to the meaning this encounter held for both of them, but I could witness what the sacred texts describe as the most intimate of all human relationships, that between guru and disciple. Relationships between parents and children, or between husband and wife, last for a lifetime, but the texts teach that guru and disciple are bound together by a vow that lasts forever.

I ended up chauffeuring Trungpa to the Black Crown ceremony, and he invited me to come to Boulder, Colorado, that summer. He told me about his vision of establishing an institute that would apply Tibetan Tantric principles to psychology, the arts, education, and other fields. I was welcome, he said, to come and continue my Tibetan language studies. I promised myself that I would go.

Legend has it that the Karmapa's fabled Black Crown is woven from the hair of one hundred thousand *dakinis*, female, sky-dwelling deities, one of whom I'd encountered years before in Nepal, so I was especially intrigued.

Accompanied by long horns, drums, and sonorous chanting, the Karmapa recited blessings, and all the while he held his hat lest it fly off his head and go back to the *dakini* realm in the sky.

The crown is said to have been a gift to the Fifth Karmapa Lama by the fifteenth-century Chinese Emperor Yung Li. The emperor had a vision of the guru's aura and had China's finest artisans replicate his vision in the physical realm, resulting in the famous Black Crown. Every Karmapa Lama since has performed this ceremony, and the crown symbolizes the power of compassion. Sadly, after the death of the Sixteenth Karmapa, disputes about his succession had to be adjudicated in Indian courts, and the young Seventeenth has not yet enacted this ritual; the crown is said to be stored away under lock and key at Rumtek.

I accepted Trungpa Rinpoche's invitation and set off for Boulder the next summer. And what a singular summer 1974 turned out to be, reminiscent of Haight-Ashbury in 1967. Naropa's faculty included eminent academic Tantra scholars, such as Herbert V. Guenther and Agehananda Bharati; famous writers, such as Allen Ginsberg and William Burroughs; as well as the composer John Cage, freelance guru Ram Dass, and a host of other counterculture icons. It was a wild scene, with nearly as many shenanigans as San Francisco had witnessed seven years before.

I returned to Philadelphia and resumed graduate studies, spent two years in Sri Lanka and India on a Fulbright, and returned in 1978 to work intensely on my dissertation. I defended it before the university committee in November, and after a night of celebrating, the very next day I flew to New Orleans for the annual meeting of the American Academy of Religion, where colleges hold a preliminary round of interviews for faculty positions. I had several interviews that resulted in several offers, but while I was waiting to hear about those opportunities, Reggie called to offer me a teaching position at Naropa, and I accepted it.

The only problem was that at just that time I was developing strong attachments in Philadelphia. For one thing, I had just met Ellen Goldberg, the woman who was to become my wife and life partner. She worked as a copy editor of a political science journal published at Temple University, where my brother Ellis was a professor—so Ellen and I were "properly" introduced by my elder brother. Her long curly brown hair and crooked smile attracted me, but most of all it was the intelligence and humor that shined through her large hazel eyes that sealed the deal, so to speak. Ellen and I decided that I should go to Boulder, and if our love was true, it would outlast the separation. In the meantime, we would call daily and visit monthly, both of which would tax our meager salaries beyond limit.

For another thing, I was learning Jewish mystical texts with Reb Zalman Schachter-Shalomi, also a professor at Temple. I had been the graduate student representative on the search committee that ended up hiring Zalman, known to be a Kabbalist and a master in the classroom. His glasses perched crookedly on his bulbous nose and his clothes made him out to be the eccentric Hasidic hippie he was and still is. But it was his resonant belly laugh, razor-sharp intellect, and encyclopedic knowledge of Judaic texts that won him the job. Zalman offered not only a path to practicing Jewish mysticism, or Kabbalah, but also the rare chance to study its texts with a truly knowledgeable master. I was just reconnecting to my Judaism and didn't want to break this tenuous link. So I asked Zalman what I should do, and he told me to go to Boulder. "It will be good for your meditation," he said. Years later, I was able to play a role in securing the World Wisdom Professorship at Naropa for him, a position he occupied until he retired.

Part of the appeal that Naropa held for me was the chance to join Trungpa's inner circle, known as the Nalanda Translation Committee. We would work on Tantric texts together, and I would teach the Pali and Sanskrit traditions in Naropa's department of Buddhist studies. It was another offer I couldn't refuse, so I was off to the Rockies.

The *Bodhisattva* Path

Predictably, under such tutelage and in such a community, my meditation practice flourished. Under Trungpa, I took what are known as "the *bodhisattva* vows." The *bodhisattva*, or "enlightenment-hero," is a Northern (Mahayana) Buddhist derivative drawn from the texts. Based on the career (*yana*) through which Siddhartha Gautama became a Buddha, it cultivates the qualities of patience, energy, equanimity, wisdom, generosity, pedagogic skill, and, mostly, compassion, through practicing meditation and carrying out kind, skillful actions in the world.

I had already begun such practices back in Dharamsala. One in particular enchanted me, the meditation known as "exchanging one's happiness for others' sufferings." In meditation, one imagines that with each out-breath, one relinquishes one's own happinesses and gives them to others, and on each in-breath one absorbs others' sufferings. I always found this particularly powerful and effective in generating compassion for "all sentient beings," which is what the Buddhist practitioner is trying to accomplish. In Boulder, I confirmed this aspiration with the ritual of the *bodhisattva* vow, which was outlined by the seventh-century Indian Buddhist poet Shantideva, one of my favorite mystical writers ever, and adapted by Trungpa. The liturgy says:

> The sufferings of others are as numerous as the grains of sand along the banks of the River Ganga, but I vow to assume them all. Sentient beings are as numerous as the stars in space, and I vow to rescue them all. The teachings (dharmas) are infinite, and I vow to master them all, for the benefit of sentient beings.

To culminate the ceremony, the guru bestows a *bodhisattva* name on the person who has completed the vow. Trungpa painted a calligraphy for me on the spot with the name "Divine Light of Intellect." It still hangs in my home.

As part of the *sangha* (Buddhist community) in Boulder, I occasionally had one-on-one interviews with the guru. I have come to learn that such intimacy is found in many esoteric paths. Hasidism has the *yehidut*, an intimate form of spiritual teaching between a rebbe and his student. The term, which means "unity" or "intimacy," also applies to the intimacy between bride and groom on the wedding night.

Zen has the *mondo*, the seemingly formal interview between a teacher and a disciple during an intensive meditation retreat, where the student reflects on a *koan*, or Zen riddle. During the *mondo*, the student presents his or her understanding of the *koan* to the *roshi* (Zen master), who either confirms that the student has "got it," that is, has attained the glimpse of enlightenment known as *satori*, or, much more likely, rebukes the student for superficiality or arrogance. The BBC educational video *Land of the Disappearing Buddha* has an absolutely wonderful example of such an exchange that many professors, including myself, use in university classes.

During a one-on-one interview, Trungpa admonished me to observe the Jewish Shabbat. "That," he said, "should be a meditation practice for you." I have no idea whether he gave other Jewish students similar counsel, or whether it was meant for me alone, or where he came up with the notion. But it began to sink in, finally, that this world was not what I had anticipated. Here was my rebbe telling me to do more Buddhist meditation, and here was my lama telling me to keep Shabbat. Who would have imagined?

More Scandals

While I was at Naropa, a scandal broke out. *Ramparts* magazine published a lengthy exposé by Peter Marin entitled "Spiritual Obedience," in which he charged that Trungpa's Boulder setup was in essence a mindless cult. Marin had taught investigative journalism at Naropa, and the community shared a strong sense of betrayal.

It made me, and everyone else there, think. To everyone's credit, the community did not dismiss Marin's charges out-of-hand. Based on what I knew of the guru-disciple relationship from Tantric texts, I drafted a lengthy rebuttal of Marin's case. *Ramparts* wouldn't publish it, but the *Vajradhatu Sun*, the *sangha* newspaper, featured it prominently. Everyone in Boulder loved my rejoinder. I defended Trungpa, but more to the point I tried to pick apart the very notion of a "cult."

I argued that, in the absence of obvious abuse, no one on the outside was in a position to understand this relationship any more than one can really understand what goes on between a husband and a wife. People have their unique ways of relating to each other in private based on a nearly infinite set of predispositions, personal histories, psychological tendencies, and the like. And if the texts—not only Buddhist or Hindu texts, but mystical texts from Kabbalah, Sufism, Christian monasticism, and more—are to be taken at their word, then the teacher-student relationship is even more intimate, making it, therefore, even more impossible for outsiders to pass judgment. I argued that in the absence of anyone's ability to offer a clear, precise definition of what is meant by a "cult," the concept is really no more than theological name-calling. Finally, I concluded, every mystical tradition is about overcoming ego or selfishness as a prerequisite for openness to the Divine: "not my will but Thy will." Therefore, what might appear to the outsider as domination or psychological terror could be, when skillfully applied, an essential spiritual technique that appears in one form or another in every esoteric tradition history has known.

A Peccadillo Here, Another Scandal There

I still believe what I wrote then, but ghosts from my childhood were soon to haunt me. While it had nothing to do with the incident that formed the basis for Marin's essay, it disturbed me deeply. Rumors abounded about Trungpa's sexual involvements with many of his female students. Having gained the trust of many in the *sangha* because of my defense against the *Ramparts* article, I asked one of Trungpa's innermost students point-blank whether these rumors were true. Probably my youthful disillusionment with my rabbi lurked not too far beneath my consciousness, and I felt heartbroken by the reply: "Rinpoche teaches from the tip of his penis."

I felt an almost personal betrayal. More than that, I felt profoundly confused. Here was a teacher of dazzling insight. His discourses remain profound. For example, just read the "Shunyata" chapter of his book, *Cutting Through Spiritual Materialism*. I found Trungpa more than brilliant; his mind had that rare quality found occasionally among spiritual masters to get behind the question posed by the questioner, to peer as it were into his or her very soul. More than once when I asked him a question and received what seemed like an off-the-wall reply, I found on reflection that his response turned out, indeed, to be addressed to the deeper question-behind-the-question. It is a phenomenon similar to mind reading, but it is no parlor game. The issues involved are existential ones; matters, as the Christian theologian Paul Tillich might have put it, of "ultimate concern." I just didn't understand how someone of such spiritual profundity could behave with such moral recklessness. The usual answer bandied around Boulder, that this was, after all, *Tantric* Buddhism, just didn't wash with me. It still doesn't.

What I have learned since then is even more depressing. Such behavior is not at all uncommon; on the contrary, it is more the rule than the exception. We know too much about the sexual abuse of children by trusted, indeed beloved, Catholic priests, and we rightly recoil in revulsion. The more I learned about spirituality, the more I came to know about rabbis, priests, swamis, Zen masters, *shuyukh*, and the like becoming sexually involved with those over whom they exert authority. Nowadays, it seems that we hear weekly of some scandal about schoolteachers molesting their students, or perverted pop stars, or professors, or psychotherapists. But the commonality of such behavior is no excuse for it. I was totally shaken.

I have to fall back upon other texts from the Tantric Buddhist tradition, many of which teach that the guru must somehow combine the mind of a Tantrika (an adept of esotericism), the altruistic motivation of a *bodhisattva*, and the behavior of a strict Theravada monk. I hold by this teaching, not because I wish to be overly moralistic, but because I have seen too often the spiritual and psychological damage that holy people can do when they act in an unholy way. Trungpa himself invented the wise concept of "spiritual materialism" to indicate the ego's ability to convert anything to its own selfish goals, even wisdom, even spirituality. It is an all-too-human failing among those we assume to be more than human.

My family recently spent our summer vacation in a cabin in the Rockies, hiking, rafting, horseback riding, and fishing. We visited with our dear friends Judith and Richard Brown, both Naropa professors, in Boulder for a couple of days, and I was most heartened to see how Trungpa's project had matured. The wooly edges had fallen away, and his "Shambhala Buddhism" institutions and community were shining brightly. Trungpa's mind had always been creative and given to synthesis, and now I see that despite his early foibles, he taught a path that remains especially appropriate for our culture. He emphasized the dignity of everyday life, a way of living in full appreciation and awareness of the elevation of the mundane. Just as the practice of Buddhist meditation has transformed many individuals, so Shambhala-oriented families, businesses, and Naropa University have transformed Boulder from a pretty college town to a unique cultural treasure.

Farewell, Boulder

Probably my real motivation for leaving Boulder was that experimental, private Naropa could not afford to pay me a living wage. But my disillusionment also came into play in my decision to accept an offer to become an assistant professor of religion at Williams College in the Berkshire Mountains of western Massachusetts. As soon as the academic year concluded, I headed off to Williamstown and a new chapter.

9

White Bread Land
Williamstown, Massachusetts

~

Founded in 1793, Williams College is generally regarded as one of the finest, most selective schools in the United States. Not long after I arrived in Boulder, I was flown to the Williams campus in the beautiful Berkshire Mountains of western Massachusetts for an interview; the beauty and charm of the place was overwhelming. The campus is an archetype of all that a liberal arts college promises to be. Later, Ellen and I used to joke that lesser schools would use the Williams campus for their catalogue illustrations.

Before too long, an offer arrived, and it was another that I couldn't refuse. After all, this was my dream, teaching Buddhism and Hinduism in stately classroom buildings nestled in maple-tree-covered hills. I had enjoyed Naropa, especially the close friendships I made, and when I left, I planned to return during the summers as a visiting professor, which I did. But Williams was undoubtedly a professional upgrade, we would be closer to family (Ellen hails from Boston), and we could make frequent trips to New York City, which was just a three-hour drive away. So it was, as they say, a no-brainer.

But early in my first semester, my dream was shaken. "Katz is a Jewish name," my new and intimidating chairman told me. "We'd like you to teach Modern Jewish Thought. Can you handle it?" The words "Of course, sir" were out of my mouth before I had even a moment to reflect. At that point in my life, that would have been my response to anything my chairman asked me. (Funny, when I was the Religious Studies chair at FIU, I didn't seem to inspire such fear in the assistant professors in my department.)

We agreed that I would teach Modern Jewish Thought during the fall semester of my second year. So while I taught Chandrakirti and Shankaracharya (seminal Buddhist and Hindu thinkers, respectively) by day, I read Abraham Joshua Heschel and Joseph Soloveitchik by night, readying myself for the next fall. The irony is that I loved what I was reading. For the first time, I read seriously about the Holocaust and Zionism. Isaac Bashevis Singer's stories enthralled me; Elie Wiesel inspired me; and I was happy to return to Martin Buber's *I and Thou*, which I had so enjoyed learning from Maury Friedman when I was an undergraduate at Temple. When autumn came, I loved teaching that course as much as I have ever loved teaching anything.

Professors, perhaps all professionals, whether consciously or not, arrange their offices to tell visitors something about themselves. It is a way of making a first impression, of establishing an identity. Books and magazines that seem casually strewn about are more revealing than one might think. So on the table in my office, colleagues and students couldn't help but notice *Oz veShalom*, an Orthodox peace activist magazine from Israel, Dharamsala's *The Tibet Journal*, on whose editorial board I have served for decades, and *Palestinian Perspectives*, a pro-PLO journal. I felt myself to be somewhat knowledgeable about Islam, since I spoke Dari and had studied with al-Faruqi in Philadelphia and Rabbani in Kabul, not to mention a variety of Sufi teachers.

I envisioned myself as a kind of bridge between Jews and Muslims, and while I never accepted al-Faruqi's view that Israel ought to cease to exist, like many liberals I wrote off such talk as mere rhetoric. Of course, I was wrong on that point, but even though I am staunchly pro-Israel these days, I remain engaged with a number of Muslims, including several imams in South Florida. Today, however, my understanding is that dialogue requires an honesty that does not gloss over real disagreements or pander to sentimentality. The problem, as I see it, is that those who are unfamiliar with the Muslim world make the mistake that just because their interlocutor is charming and gracious, he must be moderate. Over cups of mint tea, the *naïf* grants every benefit of the doubt to the Muslim dialogue partner, assuming he is amenable to compromise, and that bellicose statements are mere bombast. For Jews and for Israel, this mistake could prove fatal; such is my fear.

During the time I was at Williams, one of the issues de jour was divestment from South Africa. "Progressive" faculty and students believed that investing some of Williams' substantial endowment funds in companies that did business in South Africa was tantamount to support for the racist system of apartheid. Conservatives argued back that America's very engagement with the government there, whether political, cultural, or economic, was our best option for ameliorating apartheid and eventually encouraging South Africa to transform itself into a multiracial and open society.

I actively supported the student pro-divestment activists. One day they held a rally to coincide with a board of trustees' meeting, and as the members of the board were leaving the administration building, I was there with the students, holding a pro-divestment sign and parroting slogans. For an instant, my eyes met those of a board member, and while I did not know for sure what he was thinking, I could feel his contempt. I unexpectedly felt a sense of deep shame.

The dominant intellectual trends of the day were radical feminism and deconstructionism. I learned to feel ashamed of my maleness (just as I had been ashamed of my Jewishness when I first visited Israel), and I even co-taught a course on feminism with my good friend, the feminist philosopher Rosemarie Tong, also a graduate of Temple.

I recall a class in my religion and literature course when we were discussing feminist-lesbian critiques of Sigmund Freud's method of literary criticism. Our text was from an explicitly lesbian perspective, upholding the dictum that all heterosexual sex is rape, and that the institution of marriage is but a warrant for violation. This was the vogue, part of the radical backlash against a long history of discrimination, but it went too far.

It was parents' day, and a couple of my students' mothers and fathers were there. I was lost in my own rhetoric when, again, my eyes met those of one of the horrified parents, and I felt the same shame. Upon reflection over the years, I have come to understand that sense of shame as a voice from within my own psyche, telling me that I didn't have any idea what I was talking about, that I was simply following intellectual fashion rather than really thinking things through.

Similarly, the fad of the year in the humanities was Jacques Derrida's deconstructionism. Looking back, I am not at all sure I ever really understood why so many people admired him, but to climb the academic ladder one must go with the flow, as we used to say, and I even wrote a paper comparing Chandrakirti with Derrida.[1] The paper served me well professionally; I even was invited to present it at the University of Vienna. But today I truly doubt it had any value beyond advancing my career.

Despite all my attempts to fit in, I remained rather alienated at Williams, not for any high-minded reason, but because I felt jealous of the wealth and privilege that abound there. An example: I became friends with the so-called black dean, a fine woman named Mary Kenyatta who was from West Chester, an industrial town near Philadelphia. When I told her I was from Camden, we

---

[1] "Prasanga and Deconstruction: Tibetan Hermeneutics and the Yana," *Philosophy East and West* 34, no. 2 (1984): 185–204.

With Ven. Nyanaponika Mahathera at his Forest Hermitage,
Kandy, Sri Lanka, 1976. Considered one of the most erudite
monks in the Theravada Buddhist world, Nyanaponika was
originally a German Jew.

With Morarji Desai, Prime Minister of India, New Delhi, 1978. Leader of India's center-right
government during the late 1970s, Desai was considered a strong moral presence and a Hindu
traditionalist.

Temple University graduation, 1979. Photograph courtesy of Temple University Media Office.

With poet Allen Ginsberg, North Adams, Massachusetts, 1980. Photograph by Ellen S. Goldberg. The "poet laureate of the Beat Generation," Ginsberg was a senior student of Trungpa Rinpoche and founding chair of the Jack Kerouac School of Disembodied Poetics at his Naropa University.

With Ven. Geshe Lobsang Tenzin, Tampa, Florida, 1989. Photograph by Ellen S. Goldberg. After attaining *the geshe lharampa* degree, the pinnacle of traditional Tibetan education, Tenzin earned a Ph.D. at Emory University, Atlanta, and currently directs the Drepung Loseling Institute while teaching at Emory. The photo is taken at Congregation Rodeph Shalom in Tampa.

His Holiness the Dalai Lama with Jewish guests, Dharamsala, India, 1990. Katz is to the Dalai Lama's immediate right. This visit was immortalized in *The Jew in the Lotus*

With Rabbi Zalman M. Schachter-Shalomi, Dharamsala, 1990. A Holocaust survivor and Lubavitcher Hasid, Schachter-Shalomi left the fold and became the chief architect of the contemporary Jewish Renewal Movement.

With His Holiness the Dalai Lama, 2004. FIU photograph by Michael H. Upright. The Dalai Lama electrified South Florida audiences during his visits in 1999 and 2004, organized chiefly by Katz.

With Rabbi Adin Steinsaltz, 2005. Photograph by James Davis, religion editor of the Ft. Lauderdale *Sun-Sentinel*. Translator of the Talmud and commentator on Kabbalah, Steinsaltz is one of the leading rabbis of the generation.

Katz, his wife Ellen S. Goldberg and son Rafael Yehiel, at the Kotel, Jerusalem, 2005.

With Sarah Cohen in Kochi, India, 2005. Cohen is the unofficial leader of Cochin's Jewish women and a principal informant for the field work behind *The Last Jews of Cochin.*

With Dr. L. N. Sharma, professor emeritus and former head of the department of philosophy, Benares Hindu University. Photo taken by Mrs. Sharma at their home in Jaipur, India.

felt a kinship, and I was a frequent dinner guest at her home. Williams professed that it was working to overcome its lily-white ethos, and wanted to attract more African-American students. Since Mary was dean of students, I volunteered to visit my alma mater, Camden High School, and talk to guidance counselors and students about opportunities at Williams. She chuckled. "Child," she told me, reverting to the dialect that made both of us feel comfortable, "*they* don't want *that* kind of black student here." I soon realized what she meant; as a matter of fact, most of the black students I taught at Williams were from much more cultured, advantaged backgrounds than I was. Despite that, many of them felt a sense of entitlement and misapplied victimization that came to bother me more and more.

I became something of a role model for alienated, politically active Jewish students at that very WASPish school. My third year at William, the faculty adviser for Hillel went on leave, and I was asked to fill in for him. So there I was, adviser to the Jewish Student Association and at the same time adviser to the Buddhist Meditation Society. I chuckle as I write this, because this unlikely pattern has replicated itself throughout my life. Today, for example, I am simultaneously an adjunct professor of Hinduism at the Hindu University of America in Orlando, and academic dean at the Chaim Yakov Shlomo College of Jewish Studies, an Orthodox rabbinic seminary in Miami Beach.

Elie Wiesel

The course I taught on Modern Jewish Thought had a deep impact on me. For one thing, it taught me that with some intensive reading, I could teach virtually anything, despite lacking real academic qualification—especially if my chairman apparently believed that all I needed was a name like Katz. For another, I became inspired by what I was teaching. The twin pillars of mainstream American Judaism—the Holocaust and Zionism—were my entrée, but going deeper I was haunted by the lyricism of Heschel and the rigor of Soloveitchik. We read Buber, Singer, and Wiesel. Working through the neo-Kabbalah of Reb Zalman Schachter and the political activism of Arthur Waskow, we took the emerging Jewish Renewal movement seriously. The course became something of an identity lynchpin for many students who shared my precarious position as Jews in this summit of WASPdom. Because I was teaching such an unorthodox reading list, the course attracted students who were even more alienated from Jewish life than I was.

One fall, we were able to bring Elie Wiesel in for a lecture, and the hall was packed. One of my favorite students, a Nigerian woman, was front and center. She was from the Ibo ethnic group, which has many members who believe that they are descended from a lost tribe of Israel, and she was unabashedly philo-Semitic. At times my eyes met the student's, and it seemed to me that Wiesel noticed this unspoken interaction. And, at times, it seemed he was speaking directly to me.

At the reception after his talk, Wiesel pulled me aside and said something about how much he appreciated my influence on my students. He asked whether I ever got to Manhattan, and scribbled down his home telephone number, saying, "Call me next time you come." I was beyond astonishment at being singled out by someone I admired so deeply. Of course, Ellen and I called him just a few weeks later, and we visited on a number of occasions. I had known him not only as the world's best-known Holocaust survivor, but also as a marvelous, profound writer. Years later, when he won the Nobel Peace Prize, I mused that perhaps the literature prize would have been even more appropriate.

But from our visits and long conversations, I came to admire Wiesel even more as a mystic and Kabbalist. I felt I could pour my heart out to him, and that his spiritual depth brewed mysterious, meaningful answers . . . maybe more suggestions than answers. One time, years later, I told him about the Jews who had traveled east and become such prominent teachers in the Buddhist and Hindu traditions, summarizing that this was too bad.

In his characteristic, mysterious way, he replied, "Maybe not." I backtracked. "Well, maybe it was not too bad for them, but surely it was too bad for the Jewish people to lose such spiritual and intelligent people," I offered, but he repeated the same "Maybe not," puzzling me even more. Seeing my consternation, he elaborated: "From what you have told me, I suspect that there may be some very deep *tikkun* ['repair'] going on. But this goes much deeper than politics. Their *tikkun* is to repair the very Jewish soul."

Even so, many years later I am not sure what he meant, even though for a time I thought I understood. *Tikkun,* literally "to repair" or "to mend," is a concept introduced by the seminal Kabbalist, Rabbi Isaac Luria. In Jewish mystical tradition, the word indicates a mysterious act that repairs this broken world of ours in ways that are not immediately apparent. Luria's theology posits a God torn by exile, a condition shared with the Jewish people, a God whose male aspect remains transcendent in heaven, but whose female, immanent aspect, once safely housed in the Holy Temple, is now estranged. Just as a groom longs for his bride, as we sing each Friday night when we welcome the Sabbath, so Hashem longs for his exiled Presence. Acts of *tikkun* somehow release "sparks" of this Presence, liberating them to soar heavenward, where they and Hashem rejoice in this reunion, a reuniting that, in Luria's Kabbalistic teachings, can be attained only through human agency, in *tikkun*. Somehow, Wiesel was telling me, Jews who "go east," even to the point of joining Hindu or Buddhist orders, might be doing a deeply mysterious *tikkun*.

Brooklyn in the Berkshires

Around this time, Ellen and I decided to marry. We had met just as I was completing my dissertation at Temple, and after I went to Boulder and then to Williamstown, the emotional (and financial!) strains of a long-distance romance became more than we could bear. We concurred that Reb Zalman and only Reb Zalman should perform the marriage. We made fitful attempts to connect at a rundown, sparsely attended synagogue in North Adams, the neighboring town where we had bought a small, lovely chalet in the hills with a splendid view of Mount Greylock.

Our wedding was a summertime neo-Hasidic road show! The powers that be at Williams let us use a grand Tudor fraternity house, and family and friends from all over the northeast joined colleagues from the college for the big event. Out-of-towners arrived in time for Shabbat, which we celebrated in the small Jewish sanctuary appropriately located in the basement of the college's church. My blue-collar Jewish family was in a bit of awe of the prim campus at first, but by the time the libations began flowing at the Saturday night (*Motza'ei Shabbat*) gala, everyone settled in for a good time. It was something of a caricature: our Jewish families scarfed hors d'oeuvres while my Williams colleagues sidled up to the bar. But it was all with good spirit, especially for my dear Uncle Dave, who had spent much of the afternoon hanging out in the pool with Reb Zalman, talking in Yiddish and drinking sweet wine.

At Reb Zalman's prompting, Ellen bought me a new *tallit* as a wedding gift. My brothers hooked it onto broomsticks to make the *huppah*, or wedding canopy, and Reb Zalman told us to use it as a covering for our nuptial bed. He explained that when a married couple makes love, there are three partners present: the husband, the wife, and Hashem. The *tallit* sanctified the union in a tangible manner. And I began to understand that Jewish mysticism is to be found right here in this world, that holiness is to be evoked not in heaven, but in what most people considered to be the mundane daily world.

The ceremony itself was one of the high points of my life, matched perhaps only by our son's bar-mitzvah many years later. As neo-Hasids, with the emphasis on the "neo," we adapted the ceremony to our spirituality. Not only did Ellen walk seven times around me, as is traditional for a bride, but in a spirit of egalitarianism I likewise circled her. Zalman sang *niggunim*, and we felt surrounded by the blessings of our loved ones. As we circled one another it felt like a spiritual corkscrew, ascending higher and higher with each round. I hadn't expected my wedding to be so spiritual, but that is because Reb Zalman was orchestrating it, and it is also because that is what Jewish mysticism is all about.

A Defining Moment

Marrying Ellen, meeting Wiesel, being married by Zalman, and delving into the new field of Jewish Studies were the highlights of my five years at Williams. But there was another defining moment. This one came shortly after Israel's 1982 incursion into Lebanon. The campus was in an uproar and a town meeting was arranged. A political science colleague asked me to represent an Israeli perspective, simply because there was no one else who would. At the time, I was critical of some of Israel's policies, and had misgivings about the Lebanon adventure in particular, but nothing prepared me for the venom of my fellow panelists. They made outrageous anti-Israel claims to cheers from the students. I can honestly say that never in my life have I felt so utterly alone as I did at that moment. I was distraught. When it was my turn to speak, I was compelled to charge my interlocutors with anti-Semitism. What else could account for the packed, hostile auditorium? Why did they reserve such vehement protests for Israel? Where I had expected moderation and dialogue, I found nothing short of hatred. A few colleagues privately thanked me for "saying what needed to be said," but none in any public way. I knew then that I would not be at Williams much longer.

10

Terrorism Up (Too) Close
Sri Lanka

~

My first sabbatical leave came while I was an assistant professor at Williams College. Sabbaticals are always welcome, of course, but this one appeared on the heels of four of the most stress-filled years of my life. Coping with the demands of launching a career in a highly competitive field while trying to adjust to a dominant culture as alien to my experience as any I'd ever encountered was all that I could handle. The thought of a year back in the lands I loved, Sri Lanka and India, sustained me for much of the ordeal.

Once upon a time in American academic culture, sabbatical leaves were routine, an "entitlement" in today's parlance. But that has changed, and they have become highly competitive. To be granted a sabbatical leave, one must submit a research proposal that university officials evaluate and rank against other proposals. I had become very interested in how Buddhism in general, and Buddhist monks in particular, related with and contributed to Singhalese society. I had become very critical of the "otherworldly" characterization of Buddhism as perpetuated by the seminal sociologist Max Weber. I came to believe that the stereotypical image of Buddhists monks as socially aloof, self-centered, forest-dwelling meditators was a distortion. While a good number of monks pursued this lifestyle, many more were engaged as teachers of children, counselors to adults, meditation instructors, and even advisers to governments. What's more, my reading of the Theravada sacred literature evidenced a keen social consciousness on the part of the Buddha and his followers. Like my role model, Colonel Olcott, I was determined to right this intellectual injustice!

During 1980, I organized and led a Williams College study tour to Sri Lanka. Our explorations included a visit to the headquarters of Sarvodaya Shramadana, a non-governmental organization committed to bringing Buddhist values to bear on the effort to create a more just, more compassionate society. *Sarvodaya* means "the uplift of all," and it is a more appropriate characterization of Buddhism's ethos than the pursuit of an otherworldly nirvana as postulated by Weber and most of modern scholarship. After all, I argued in my sabbatical proposal, Sri Lanka has a disproportionately high quality of life (as measured by the United Nations) in relation to a fairly low economic base. In short, no country had done so much for its people with such a paucity of resources. My idea was to trace this enlightened social policy to a Buddhist influence. Williams accepted my proposal, and in the summer of 1983, Ellen and I set off for Sri Lanka.

We took the opportunity to visit Italy, Turkey, Israel, Burma, and India en route, and just as we were about to embark on the last leg of our journey, all hell broke lose in Sri Lanka. Horrible communal violence between Singhalese and Tamils overwhelmed the country. When we landed in Colombo, smoke still smoldered from burned homes and factories; the roads were strewn with toppled buses; and not all of the dead had yet been buried or cremated. This paroxysm made the 1977 upheavals I had witnessed seem like child's play.

A good friend who was all smiles and laughter met us at Bandaranaike International Airport. It might have been even more unnerving to see her in such good spirits as we drove past burned vehicles and shops, but I already understood that Singhalese people tend to mask deep anxiety with chuckles and conviviality. Perhaps that is part of what Jim Gair had meant about a dark underside to a seemingly sunny self-presentation.

What had happened? What led to such horrible turmoil? How could people who had known one another all their lives, who had married into each other's families, who had been schoolmates, raise machetes and axes against each other?

Of course, tensions had been building for decades. Some would say, for centuries and more, ever since the first century B.C.E., when the great Singhalese king, Dutthagamini, defeated the Tamils, whom he had seen as encroaching upon his domain. In a jarring image from the *Mahavamsa*, an idealized history of the island written in the fifth century, King Dutthagamini affixed a relic of the Buddha to his spear as he led his armies. Ankle deep in blood, Dutthagamini felt remorse, but Buddhist monks consoled him, saying that since the Tamils were not Buddhists, no human lives had been taken—save half a life for one Tamil who was about to take refuge in the Triple Gem.

1977 All Over Again

Apparently, some Tamil militants had attacked a government military convoy in the northern, Tamil-dominated Jaffna Peninsula, resulting in the deaths of about thirty soldiers. Seemingly in spontaneous revenge, the Singhalese re-taliated, slaughtering thousands of Tamils in their homes and shops. Once the dust cleared, it seemed that these pogroms were more orchestrated than spon-taneous. But by whom?

Accusations and counter-accusations proliferated. Ill-informed western journalists checked into Colombo's best hotels for "on-the-spot" coverage, as if the Hilton were the battlefield. Before leaving Massachusetts, my wife had hooked up with the *Christian Science Monitor* as a stringer, and covering the carnage we saw was enough to make a journalist's career. And, of course, every-thing we saw was a nightmare to anyone with empathy, including my reporter-wife, who had not had the inoculation of my exposure to similar events in 1977.

As is typical of such ethnic conflicts, both sides felt aggrieved. The Sing-halese pointed to the economic structure imposed upon the island by the British, who gave the minority Tamils meager privileges in exchange for act-ing as surrogates or middlemen for the colonial rulers. The French assigned this role to the Jews in Algeria, to offer a parallel example. As the Tamils benefited from the English education provided by the missionaries, the Singhalese fell to the bottom of the social pyramid in a country they understood as theirs, a country they had traditionally called Singaladvipa, "island of the Singhalese." After independence from the British in 1948, nationalism swept through the majority of the population. In 1956, Sri Lanka (then Ceylon) elected a gov-ernment some might consider Singhalese chauvinist. Fired by rhetoric from Buddhist monks and lay leaders alike, Prime Minister Solomon W. R. D. Ban-daranaike rode a wave of Singhalese sentiment. His government declared Sin-hala to be the national language and gave Buddhism semiofficial status, resurrecting the precolonial idea that the government had the responsibility to defend Buddhism. The Singhalese felt that the Tamils had benefited at their expense, and, in short, their politics demanded that the imbalance be rectified. That was the prevailing national mood from the mid-1950s to the early 1980s.

The Tamils saw their status diminish steadily after independence, and now it was their turn to feel aggrieved. On a larger scale, while the Tamils (about a third of Sri Lanka's population) perceived themselves as a minority on the is-land, the majority Singhalese felt themselves to be a minority vis-à-vis neigh-boring India, because its southern state of Tamil Nadu, with its sixty million people, looms just a couple of dozen miles across the Palk Strait. The situation is not altogether dissimilar to the Israeli-Palestinian equation, wherein Pales-tinians view themselves as a threatened minority within Israel, while Israeli

Jews view their population of six million or so in the context of a tiny group amid 120 million hostile Arabs.

I tried to come to some conclusion as to the relative merits of the Singhalese and Tamil claims. Were Tamils underrepresented in the upper echelons of Sri Lanka's elite? Was Singhalese culture in some way under siege? Was there a right and a wrong side of the conflict? Whatever the "facts" may have been, the situation was far too volatile and fast moving to rest upon such a flimsy base, and I had just arrived.

In the wake of the pogroms, both sides took up arms. The Liberation Tigers of Tamil Eelam ("Eelam" is the name proposed for an independent Tamil state carved out of the northern and eastern parts of the island), also called LTTE or simply the Tigers, engaged in the systematic murder of any opposition within their own community before conducting less systematic attacks on the Singhalese military and government. Increasingly, terrorism became their method: they attacked schoolchildren; they blew up busses and trains carrying commuters to work; anonymous attackers exploded bombs in the country's markets. Their tactics were uncomfortably familiar: first to silence dissent within their own community, and then to attack the most vulnerable among the "enemy." The Singhalese, for their part, increasingly relied upon a military approach to the terrorist problem. Political dialogue waned. No one was even talking about a peace settlement along federalist lines.

I hastily redesigned my research project. There was no longer any possibility of discussing a Buddhist vision for Sri Lanka's society; that was a luxury that no longer existed in these desperate times. Instead, I embarked upon a series of extensive interviews with Singhalese monks to try to find out their perspectives on the ethnic conflict. While a few expressed sympathy for the "underlying causes" of the Tamil uprising, most gritted their teeth and followed a staunchly nationalist line.[1] It was not my most uplifting piece of scholarship, but it did reveal what terrorism does to people, including the people against whom it is directed.

My wife hit the journalistic jackpot reluctantly. Her newspaper welcomed her dispatches, which in the days before e-mail and fax machines had to be delivered to Boston by some compliant world traveler or survive a two-week airmail from the sub–post office in the village where we were living. Sometimes

---

[1] "Social and Political Attitudes of Sri Lankan Monks: An Empirical Study,' with F. Robert Stiglicz. *South Asia Research* 6, no. 2 (1986): 159–180.

the tiny post office didn't even have enough postage stamps for the envelope holding photographs and the story she had pounded out on our portable typewriter. The nearest teletype machine was in the Reuters building in Colombo, about four hours distant. It was fortunate for her that the *Monitor* was not oriented toward breaking news but was more interested in background studies, because that was all the antiquated communications of the day and place allowed.

In the middle of the turmoil, we traveled north by bus to Jaffna in Sri Lanka's Tamil heartland. Even on the bus, Ellen interviewed Tamils who lived and worked in Kandy or Colombo, but were returning to Jaffna to see how their families had fared through the pogroms. We visited refugee camps, our hearts aching for the new orphans and displaced, terrified people. It's the kind of turmoil made for CNN, but it is quite another matter to see, hear, smell, and touch such misery.

Through colleagues at the International Centre for Ethnic Studies, where I was doing some work, we had good contacts among the Tamil political and cultural leaders in Jaffna. They were advised that Ellen was writing for the *Christian Science Monitor*, so they rolled out the red carpet for us. Their unspoken assumption was that they would get a sympathetic hearing in a respected American newspaper. When they learned that we were Jewish, they took our sympathy for granted. Even in Jaffna, the Jewish heart's embrace of causes such as theirs was legendary.

Our local contacts took us to one of the area's leading private schools and introduced us to the headmaster, who had arranged a reception in our honor. In traditional South Asian fashion, our hosts garlanded us, which is to say placed luxuriant strings of fragrant flowers around our necks. Schoolchildren serenaded us, and the headmaster asked us to speak as representatives of sorts of the Jewish people to the Tamil people. Being placed in such an untenable position made me most uncomfortable, especially since I had not yet worked out my own understanding of their conflict.

A vegetarian dinner followed the ceremony, after which the headmaster invited us for a "secret" tour of what he called the boys' facility. We could not have imagined what this kindly, educated, refined gentleman had in mind, but, of course, we gladly acceded. Where he was taking us was to a terrorist training camp. In the middle of the night, "the boys" showed us Kalashnikovs and hand grenades, and treated us to demonstrations of camouflaging and military drills. Aghast, I asked where they had learned these techniques, and the headmaster proudly declared that the community had sent many of the boys to secret camps in South India, and had managed to send their leadership cadres to Lebanon for training by you-can-imagine-who.

Over the next few months, one after another of our Tamil friends, including several members of parliament and other relatively moderate leaders, were slaughtered in strikingly brutal ways. Not too long after, the headmaster met the same fate. I guess even he was too moderate for some of his neighbors.

I began to understand terrorism, which is to say I began to grow up. As a child of the 1960s, like numerous members of my generation, I romanticized "militants" or "freedom fighters," as we liked to call them. And, like so many of my university colleagues, I staunchly believed that their violence had "underlying causes" in oppression, and was, therefore, excusable if not heroic. What's more, I had believed that if the powers that be took the proper approach to the militants' problems and addressed their "legitimate grievances," then, somehow, the terrorism would vanish. Whether speaking of Tamils or Palestinians or other such "rebels," my ideology of liberation demanded such a naive analysis. But now that the link between Tamils and other terrorists was less abstract and all too concrete, my ideological beliefs began to crumble, slowly but surely.

One piece at a time, my experiences contradicted my liberal-leftist worldview. The conflict at hand was, in principle at least, manageable if not fully solvable. All it needed was a bit of compromise, a smidgen of good will, a lot of talking in an environment of relative calm. Incessant provocations, such as bombs in the markets and the slaughter of Buddhist monks, surely did not help. But my faulty assumption had been that people on both sides wanted a solution and sought accommodation. That is precisely where I had been wrong. And that's what I mean when I said that I was growing up. Some people don't want solutions.

My wife eventually reported on all this in the *Christian Science Monitor*. Much to the newspaper's credit, it published her reports even though they were out of sync with the newspaper's general worldview. And much to our dismay, later on, officials from the government of India also read what Ellen wrote, and they were not at all pleased, as we were to learn just a couple of years later. After all, India's government has heatedly denied the presence of Tamil terrorist bases in South India for years. It was not until Prime Minister Rajiv Gandhi encountered the world's first-known suicide-bomber (or, more aptly, "homicide-bomber") some years later that the whole sordid story came to light.

All of this, of course, reflected back upon my understanding of the Middle East. I once had thought, "If the Israelis were just a little bit more forthcoming, if only they would not subject the poor Palestinians to such hardships as roadblocks and patrols. If only they would give them their own state behind the 1949 armistice line, then all would be well." Now I began to see that once terrorism becomes legitimate, once youth are indoctrinated into a culture of violence, once twelve- and fourteen-year-old boys are trained with automatic weapons, it is too late for such rationalism. Peace-making requires, above all, moderation, willingness to compromise. As Carole King's song goes, "You can't talk to a man with a shotgun in his hand . . . You can't talk to a man when he don't want to understand. No, no, no, no, no, no." I wish someone in the UN would listen to that lyric.

On the way back to our modest hotel from the headmaster's shocking display of the juvenile terrorist training camp, Singhalese soldiers pulled our taxi over and pointed rifles in our direction. We were in the back seat as rifles appeared at each window, aimed at our skulls. The canny driver immediately switched on the overhead light, and when the soldiers saw our white faces—even whiter than usual, I'd imagine—they lowered their guns and smiles brightened the night. "Good evening, sir. Good evening, madam," the soldiers greeted us, waving us along our way.

The Peace March

The violence deeply affected people on both sides of Sri Lanka's ethnic divide. Dr. A. T. Ariyaratne, "Ari" to all, and his Sarvodaya organization were at the forefront of constructive response. Sarvodaya, which is based on Buddhist beliefs and Singhalese culture, always had an inclusive agenda. The party (movement?) selected Kataragama, a multireligious sacred complex at the island's southernmost point, as the focus for a *padayatra*, a peace march. Buddhist, Hindu, Muslim, and Christian leaders joined in, and youthful marchers from all over the nation converged upon the remote enclave, with its Buddhist *stupa*s, Hindu *kovil*s, Muslim *masajid*, and Christian churches.

We hooked up with the local Sarvodaya group in Kandy for a long, long chartered bus ride through some of the most beautiful landscapes on earth. The journey, though not the scenery, reminded me so much of the buses from Philadelphia to New York's Central Park, or to the Pentagon near Washington, that we rode as student protestors during the anti–Vietnam War demonstrations; the youthful exuberant optimism felt just the same as we sang and chatted on the way.

We had booked a room in a pilgrim rest house, the cruddiest quarters I had seen in my life—and that is saying something! As we walked around the town, we longingly gazed at the modern accommodations (which we hadn't known about), and unsurprisingly we ran into filmmaker Manik Sandrasagara relaxing over a gin and tonic at the most posh hotel. He told us that many of the most venerable monks of Sri Lanka were also staying there, and he introduced us to the Venerable Walpola Rahula, author of the best introductory book about Buddhism I have ever read, one I always use in my college courses. Manik the mystic was far from pious, and he sarcastically raved that the march, replete with robed swamis, monks, imams, and priests, was "the best show in town."

Manik introduced me to a quiet swami who lived in a very simple hut at Kataragama. The swami befriended me, and we spent much of the next several days together as he showed me around the sacred complex. He told me secrets of the cult of Subramaniyam, eldest son of Lord Shiva, who is said to reside there. He told me more secrets about the sacred architecture of the site, a map writ large of the cosmos, of human consciousness, worshipped by Hindu, Buddhist, Christian, and Muslim devotees. He described the roundabout pilgrimage routes trod by Hindu renunciates from all over the island and much of India, each step rich with symbolic and esoteric meanings.

The swami was a devotee of Lord Shiva and held to a non-dualist, Advaita viewpoint that emphasizes the oneness of the devotee and God. At the same time, he also emulated and worshipped Lord Krishna with his melodious flute. Like the west's Pied Piper, Lord Krishna summons and serenades his devotees with his flute, known as a *murali*. I saw many people ask the swami to perform, but he would play only when the spirit moved him. "I play only for the L-rd," he demurred.

After a remarkable display of rituals and numerous speeches, the march began. Thousands of people of good will joined young Sarvodaya volunteers for the trek to Tissamahara, about ten miles distant. We had barely begun walking when we spied Manik, sitting in a café drinking tea. He beckoned us over and invited us to have "just one cup, before you start walking." One cup led to another and another, and Manik kept us in stitches. He mocked the wealthy folk from Colombo who joined in the march, roaring with laughter: "What can I do?" he mimicked. "I walked all the way to Tissa, and those buggers still burned down my factory." Before we knew it, the day had passed. Manik then called for his car and had us driven to within a quarter mile of the march's end. As Ellen and I reached the end point, we came upon the young Sarvodaya workers from Kandy. They expressed their admiration that we had walked so far with them, but seemed as fresh as we had at the start. Then we joined Manik for a ride back to Colombo and its fine restaurants.

Guns and Ghee

Having rifles pointed at our heads made us a bit nervous, and the atmosphere in Sri Lanka was not exactly conducive to my research. Given that, we decided to divide the sabbatical between Sri Lanka and India, and started planning a trip from India's southern tip at Kanya Kumari, all the way up to the far side of the Himalayas, to Ladakh, a Tibetan cultural area that serendipitously had ended up on the Indian side of the border. In the religious freedom and cultural pluralism that is India, Ladakh is one of the very few places on earth with a continuous Tibetan culture.

I had long wanted to visit Cochin, a port city on the Malabar Coast of southwestern India, the hospitable home to a fabled, ancient Jewish community. We flew from Sri Lanka to Trivandrum, capital of the modern state of Kerala. Then we took a pilgrim bus tour to Kanya Kumari, which is dedicated to the Virgin Goddess and which stands where the Bay of Bengal, the Indian Ocean, and the Arabian Sea meet. From there, a backwater boat took us to Cochin.

The boat plied the tropical waters past villages and farms, providing a unique glimpse into rural life in Kerala. It was a rickety craft, and slow as well. The toilet facilities were two cubicles at the stern with walls about four feet tall and a hole in the floor. As I stood up in my cubicle, I was confronted by another foreigner who was simultaneously also just standing up. It reminded me of the famous Marx Brothers routine where Harpo and Groucho mimic one another as though they are being reflected in a mirror.

We both enjoyed the moment, laughing as he and his girlfriend joined Ellen and me for the rest of the ride. They had both recently graduated from Brown University, and they knew a number of my Williams students. We hit it off well, and I offered them some contacts to pursue in their travels. He was tall and handsome, and she was tall and beautiful, and both were bright and personable. Coincidences abound on the road, and when we got to Cochin, we were put in adjoining hotel rooms, so we toured around together.

We told them that Ellen was planning to do a feature about Cochin's Jewish community for the *Monitor*. We found the community remarkably hospitable. When we met its matriarch, Gladys Koder, she commented on something she had just read in the Malayalam-language daily newspaper. "Did you know that President Kennedy's son was in town?" she asked, showing me a grainy photograph on the front page. I didn't even have to look; that was our new friend.

This led us to a dilemma. We could appreciate that any celebrity would cherish some anonymity, so we wondered whether we should reveal that we knew who he was. We didn't want to be dishonest with our new friend, but nevertheless we decided to keep our discovery secret. One evening as we dined at a restaurant, streams of Indians came up asking for his autograph, so I imagine he knew that we knew.

As we became familiar with the Cochin Jews, they seemed to like us. One factor in our favor was that we were sincere, if not especially knowledgeable, Jews. My experiences in deep exile in Williamstown had brought my Jewishness to the surface of my consciousness. Our palpable admiration for Indian civilization was another plus. Indian Jews are very proud of both facets of their identity, though foreign Jews might be less than enthusiastic about India, or Indians might be lukewarm about Judaism. Because our identities in this sense matched theirs, we felt we were being especially welcomed.

Two facts became obvious to us. First, this community was on the verge of extinction. Emigration to Israel had reduced its numbers so that it no longer had a critical mass of people to provide ritual quorums (*minyanim*) and sufficient marriage partners for the youngsters. The fate of the community was inexorable. Second, no one had ever written a book about Cochin's Jews, and it struck us as profoundly sad that this proud community, with such a long history and so many intriguing customs, would go out of existence with nothing left to remember it by. What's more, Sara Cohen, unofficial leader of Cochin's Jewish women, urged us to be the ones to do the task. "Such a long history here," she implored, "and people are already forgetting everything. Please come back to us before it is all lost; please come back, and write about us."

This provoked long discussions with my wife about a critical career choice: whether or not to devote a couple of tenure-earning years to doing a book in Cochin. We felt this could be a good combination of our talents: hers as a journalist—she is a skilled interviewer and a very good photographer to boot—and mine as a scholar of Indian civilization who also knows something about Jewish culture. It was a great professional risk, but we decided to do it. Our minds made up, we said goodbye to our new Cochini friends and traveled northward, intending to return with more background and a nice research grant as soon as we could.

Parallel Exiles

Later in our India sojourn, Ellen and I visited Drepung Loseling Monastery, a leading Tibetan college that has been rebuilt in remote, impoverished Mundgod in South India's Karnataka state. We arrived during the season for the Great Prayer Festival, the Mön-lam Chen-mo, instituted in the fifteenth century by the great spiritual leader Tsong Khapa. My research kept me in the monastery's library, and, naturally enough, I became friendly with the librarian, an earnest, unassuming monk. One day we were discussing how an exiled people could maintain its traditions in alien lands. What he said amazed me. "We take our cue from the Jews. They lost their homeland, but despite so much hardship and suffering, they maintained their culture. We must learn from them," he said, entirely unaware that he was addressing a Jew. Some years later, I read and translated a pamphlet by Jamyang Norbu, one of Tibet's most fiery exiled leaders. He had published the essay to commemorate a nationalist day in Tibetan history, and it was entitled *An Outline of the History of Israel.* Page after page lauded Jewish determination, courage, intelligence, and fidelity to tradition—the precise virtues most needed by an exiled community. The writer reserved his highest praises for the most militant Zionists, the so-called Stern Gang. I began to realize that just as fast as many Jews were running toward Buddhism, many Tibetans were trying to emulate Jews.[2] I wondered what the conversation might be if and when their paths crossed. I was to find out, years later.

Since I had known him for some years, Ellen hoped to interview the Dalai Lama when we went to Dharamsala, but her Boston editors were skeptical. They told her that their New Delhi bureau chief had been trying to schedule an interview with him for years, but with no luck. I knew Dharamsala better, I thought, and what was needed was patience. I somewhat overconfidently promised Ellen that we could get an interview with him if we just showed up, asked politely, and waited. Anyway, I reasoned, there was plenty to do and see while there; it is a beautiful place with great hikes and extensive cultural life. She got the interview, and her editors were surprised and pleased.[3]

While strolling Dharamsala's market, I saw a new institution, the Museum of the Tibetan Holocaust. It was very crude, just some photos and memorabilia, but the intent was obvious: to document Chinese atrocities in Tibet and to memorialize the one million–plus Tibetans, of a total population of around six million, who had died as a consequence of the occupation. Since then, the Tibetans have upgraded the museum significantly with the aid of staff members from Jerusalem's Yad Vashem Holocaust Memorial, and while

---

[2] Nathan Katz, trans., " 'A Tibetan-Language *History of Israel* by Jamyang Norbu." *Journal of Indo-Judaic Studies* 1 (1998): 81–89.

[3] Ellen S. Goldberg and Nathan Katz, "Tibet's Exiled Leader Talks of Homeland Now Ruled by China," *Christian Science Monitor,* July 30, 1984.

not exactly state of the art, the memorial is effective as well as aesthetically pleasing.

Not far from there is the office of the Tibetan Youth Congress (TYC), a social and political group with huge influence in the exile community. The TYC has been known to advocate military resistance to the Chinese occupation and is generally inclined toward the radical end of the Tibetan political spectrum. In assuming this stance, it conflicts with the Dalai Lama's insistence on nonviolence. On this visit, I saw something that was new to me: a banner hung on the building's facade that read "Next Year in Lhasa." Clearly, Tibetans had learned about us Jews, and I became all the more intrigued to explore this intercultural phenomenon. Inspired by such synchronization, I was also rediscovering my Jewishness, albeit in a secular sense.

Starting Over in America

In New Delhi, we stayed at the YMCA Tourist Hostel. When Ellen spoke with her editor in Boston and told him where we were, I think it took five very costly intercontinental telephone minutes for him to stop laughing. Journalists generally lead a more luxurious life.

One day we received a cable from my brother Ellis. The cable read: "USF wants to interview you for a job. Can you return quickly?" We thought, "San Francisco, how wonderful!" When we finally were able to get a phone call through, much to my chagrin I learned that USF meant University of South Florida rather than of San Francisco, and the school was in Tampa. Well, we were ready for a change, so we cut our Indian idyll short. Back in the States, I interviewed and got the offer. We sold our pretty little chalet in the Berkshires and headed south.

Life was pleasant in the Sunshine State, but no sooner had we arrived than we began planning our return to Cochin.

11

Pukkha Cochinites
Cochin

~

Less than two years later, we were on our way back to Cochin, supported by another Fulbright. I was now on leave from the University of South Florida in Tampa.

But there was a major glitch on the journey. The government of India was very slow about approving our research project, which meant that our residency visas could not be granted, which in turn meant that our Fulbright stipend could not be implemented. After many discussions with the Council for the International Exchange of Scholars, the agency that runs Fulbright programs, we were assured that while the delay was mysterious, it shouldn't be a problem. Our proposal was entirely uncontroversial, and approval would just be a matter of time. While the council could not purchase our air tickets without India's approval, we ought to go ahead and buy them, and we'd be reimbursed later.

In any case, we had to pack up and put our stuff into storage. I took an unpaid leave from the university, my wife resigned her job as an editor for a Tampa lifestyle magazine, and we were off. We decided to wait out the visa in Nepal during its prime festival season, which was a pleasant enough prospect, and more or less in the neighborhood. So we waited and waited, remaining in close contact with both the Indian embassy and United States Educational Foundation there. Our money began to run short, and we became increasingly anxious. Our plan was to document the ritual life of the Cochin Jews, and Rosh Hashanah was approaching, so we simply couldn't wait. We entered India on tourist visas and headed for Cochin, keeping in touch this time with the U.S. Educational Foundation in New Delhi.

We wrote home about our visa problems, as well as our growing financial anxieties. At this point, I could not return to the university at least until the spring semester, and it was now or never for our research. My mother-in-law, Bunny Fuchs, bless her soul, pretty much camped out at Senator Ted

Kennedy's Boston office to try to enlist support. She repeatedly called the Indian embassy in Washington, pleading our case. She even sent the ambassador her homemade brownies. Certainly the U.S. Educational Foundation did all it could, but all to no avail. If seemed a Kafkaesque situation. We love India, and we knew—even if we might be suspected—that we were not spies or the like, and we also intended to write a book that was to be entirely laudatory of India's hospitality to her Jews. So why weren't we getting our visas? Then one day a fateful telegram arrived from New Delhi: "With deep regret, we have to inform you that the Government of India has disapproved your visa."

We wrote letters to everyone we could think of, asking for help, including Elie Wiesel, who had just been awarded the Nobel Peace Prize. We were busily documenting religious observances in Cochin, and then one day, out of the blue, everything reversed. Our visa was approved, and the council told us to come right away to New Delhi for orientation. When we got there, of course, the biggest question on our minds was, What happened? Why was our research first rejected, and later mysteriously approved? An official at the American embassy told us that its staffers were equally puzzled; they had never seen such a reversal, which they learned had come from the highest possible level, meaning the prime minister's office. I put two and two together, and concluded that Wiesel must have telephoned Rajiv Gandhi, who gave the word to his underlings. While I have never been able to confirm my hypothesis, I can think of no other plausible explanation. The embassy folks agreed that such a remarkable shift at South Block, the building complex in New Delhi that houses the prime minister's office and the most important government ministries, made Gandhi's personal involvement plausible.

Settling into Cochin Life

Soon after we got to Cochin, we learned that the community had held a meeting about us. They decided to facilitate our efforts, and invited us to move in with one of the families on Synagogue Lane in Jew Town. Having such unrestricted access and being so accepted was an anthropologist's dream. We knew we would be forced to give up most creature comforts, including much-coveted air-conditioning and privacy, but it was yet another offer we couldn't refuse. And so for a year, we ate, prayed, and socialized with this otherwise closed community, becoming, in their words, "*pukkha* Cochinites," which might be freely translated as "members of the tribe."

We visited every synagogue in South Asia, meeting community members and praying daily. I came to love the Indian-Sephardic chants and prayers. For the first time in either of our lives, our personal rhythms became synchronized with the Jewish calendar. We lived the life of observant Jews as part of immersing ourselves in the participant-observer anthropological method.

As the weeks and months passed, we felt more and more absorbed into the community. I prayed with the men; Ellen worked in the homes with the women, camera ever ready. A husband-and-wife team is the perfect instrument for doing this type of fieldwork in a traditional community. In traditional societies, men and women do different things, and male and female researchers who can combine their efforts seamlessly are needed to get any sort of holistic understanding of the community.

I also came to a new understanding of personal space. What we in America call privacy would in India be considered loneliness. People felt free to walk into any room in a neighboring home, and all of the houses are connected on the second story. Synagogue Lane is so narrow that you can easily converse with a neighbor across the street while sitting comfortably in your own upstairs parlor. I had a long-standing nostalgia for the community in Camden, but this was something else again!   .

Both Ellen and I were struck by the impact of praying in the beautiful synagogue. Ellen told me that the women chanted prayers enthusiastically and knowledgbably in their upstairs section. Whenever they could not hear the prayer leader downstairs, or if they felt he was praying too rapidly with insufficient inner intention (*kavvanah*), the women displayed no reticence about calling out their displeasure, demanding louder or slower, chants, or occasionally correcting a mispronounced word. The men swayed gently and prayed sweetly. One morning I heard Jacob Cohen call out a correction to the congregant reading the Torah, and when I glanced his way I saw that he had no book on his lap. He was correcting entirely from memory.

As it is supposed to be, Yom Kippur was the summit of the High Holy Days. The scene was so beautiful when we arrived for *Kol Nidrei*: a white curtain (*parokhet*) hung before the *Aron ha-Kodesh* (the cabinet or Ark holding the Torah scrolls), everyone was wearing white clothes, each oil lamp had a burning wick, and the sun's setting rays suffused into a pinkish sheen on every surface.

The next day, as ceiling fans lazily spun and bats flew from chandelier to chandelier, the men would occasionally sprawl on a window seat for some fresh air or a brief rest during the long service. But not the women. Ellen told me that the custom is for women to stand throughout the entire day, from dawn until after sunset. Since many of the women were elderly, and managed to stand all day anyway, Ellen felt she had no choice but to stand. By the evening *Ne'ilah* service, just before the *shofar* blast that would herald the fast's end, she told me she had a sense of exhilaration, of closeness to God, that she had never before experienced. I knew that we had entered the community not only physically but spiritually.

From Participant-Observers to Observant Jews

I was caught unaware by what came next. I didn't anticipate what this year was doing to me internally. Without my conscious knowledge, Judaism had crept into my bones. Our research done, and deeply fond farewells exchanged, we left Cochin. En route to Israel to interview Cochin Jews who had resettled there, we spent a couple of weeks in Bombay, or Mumbai as it is now called. I was looking forward to visiting the fine restaurants there; in particular, I had been lusting after shrimp, which I had not tasted for a year. We sat down and opened our menus. My eyes leaped to the seafood section. But I just couldn't do it! I couldn't bring myself to order such blatantly nonkosher food. I was thoroughly taken aback. I hadn't known what was happening to me.

During that visit to Bombay, we came to know Ben and Sally Afif, an elderly Baghdadi couple who were mentors to many young Jews. Ben taught us a lesson I have never forgotten, although I am sure he was completely unaware of having such a significant impact. It was so simple really. He ceremonially washed his hands, and then recited the appropriate *berakhah* before enjoying the Shabbat meal. There is nothing unusual about that; observant Jews do it several times a day before eating. But it was the way he recited it that made such a lasting impression. His eyes rolled upward as he toweled his hands, and with a sweet, sweet smile, he slowly intoned the words: "Blessed art Thou, O Lord our God, King of the universe, Who has sanctified us with Thy commandments, and commanded us to lift up our hands." So simple, so utterly unremarkable. And so deeply moving.

A Surprising New Path

Our stay in Israel made a deep impression on both of us. Although it was not our first time there together, our spiritual connections were of an altogether different order. Before, we had felt like tourists most of the time. Now we felt the connection, the sense of belonging, that many Jewish pilgrims have described over the centuries.

One of the challenges facing us when we returned to Tampa was how to maintain the spiritual level we had attained in India and Israel. The other challenge was, of course, writing our book, which took two years. We are proud of our collaborative effort and the requiem we created for the dwindling Cochin Jewish community.[1]

We joined a Conservative synagogue and enjoyed it thoroughly. I reverted to my childhood role as prayer leader, at least for the preliminary service, occasionally entertaining the congregants with an Indian melody. Since I am not gifted with a good singing voice, I had to focus intently to stay on tune. So before Saturday morning services I would retire to the chapel, wrap myself in my *tallit*, and meditate for fifteen or twenty minutes. I found that by practicing mindfulness, I could navigate the liturgy's intricate melodies satisfactorily.

After a while, some of the congregants, especially the older ones, asked me what I was doing in the chapel. When I told them I was meditating to warm up for praying, they asked whether I would teach them how. So for the next year or so, I found myself teaching *vipassana* for half an hour before leading the prayers.

At the same time, my wife, who had been raised with very little Judaic background, was learning Hebrew and catching up on decades of learning. It is remarkable how motivation can hasten such a process.

After two years in our comfortable religious niche, a television news program intruded with the horrible image of a United Airlines plane pinwheeling in a fiery crash in Iowa. An hour or two later the news came by telephone: our beloved rabbi and his wife, Kenny and Aviva Berger, had been killed in the maelstrom. Kenny was around my age, hailed from Philadelphia, and had studied at Temple University. Kenny and Aviva were friends, and this was the first time Ellen or I had ever lost a contemporary. The loss of friends and the loss of one's clergyman blended in this gut-level encounter with death and changed both of us.

Kenny's most eloquent sermon had been right after the *Challenger* spacecraft disaster. In fact, Ellen was watching the launch at Cape Canaveral from her magazine office on Tampa Bay when the spacecraft exploded. The next Saturday, Kenny asked us to imagine what it would be like if we knew for certain that we were just minutes from certain death. His rhetorical question was whether it was death that we feared, or was it that we hadn't really lived to the fullest. That was just three years before he had to confront the question himself.

---

[1] *The Last Jews of Cochin: Jewish Identity in Hindu India* (Columbia: University of South Carolina Press, 1993).

Our Bout with Cancer

Around this time, my wife and I decided it was high time to start a family. Actually, she had wanted a baby for several years and, typical male, I dragged my feet. Having made the decision, pregnancy wasn't so simple as we had blithely expected. The joy we felt when we learned we were pregnant was dashed when Ellen suffered a miscarriage. We tried for another pregnancy, but to no avail. Failed efforts became increasingly sad, frustrating, and bewildering. As a card-carrying member of the baby boomer "have it your way" generation, things were not going according to plan. I felt entitled to a child when I wanted one, and it simply never occurred to me that it wouldn't happen that way.

As months passed, our inability to conceive invaded our minds and hearts at every turn. We envied our friends pushing strollers. We could no longer look at maternity books we'd snatched up the year before. And we railed at the injustice of life whenever we read about a crack-addled teen mother who abandoned her child, or worse.

As Judaism became more entrenched in our lives, we felt left out of God's divine plan that humans be parents. Children are part of the spiritual lot of Judaism, and as a twosome we felt a mockery. Well-meaning friends sensed this. After making the blessing of bread at a Shabbat meal we shared with one couple—the parents of three adorable children—they reserved the end piece of the *challah* in the traditional belief that this assists a woman trying to conceive.

In the synagogue, I found myself looking longingly at the toddlers who scrambled along when their fathers were called up to recite the blessing of the Torah. For both Ellen and me, one of the most heart-rending moments was the recitation of *Hallel*, or "Praises," a series of psalms recited in synagogues on holidays to commemorate God's many miracles.

After a blessing, Psalm 113 is recited, and it concludes with these verses:

> He raises the needy from the dust, from the trash heaps He lifts the destitute.
> To seat them with nobles, with the nobles of His people.
> He transforms the barren wife into a glad mother of children.
> Halelu-kah!

Standing beside my wife in the Conservative synagogue, I felt her doleful gaze as we recited, each of us choking back sobs. And then one day, as we came to the last line, she bolted out of the sanctuary.

When I caught up with her outside, we shared our feelings of loss—we both wanted a child, but even in that painful moment I knew her pain was more direct. Mine was contaminated by my egoistic sense of entitlement. She wanted a baby. And we both grieved for our very sense of place within the family-centered path of Judaism.

Eventually, we embarked on a torturous two-year round of fertility treatments, to the extent that medical technology and our meager finances would allow. Like others who have been through this, it was a challenge to our intimacy and well-being as a couple. Ultimately, our physician suggested that my wife undergo exploratory laproscopic surgery in the hopes of identifying the problem so he could better treat it. He described the outpatient procedure as so routine that we scheduled it on our anniversary and made reservations at a kosher hotel in Miami Beach for a little Sabbath R&R.

The waiting time extended hour after hour, and I became increasingly anxious. After what seemed like an eternity, our doctor, still in surgical scrubs, found me. He told me the grim news. They had found cancer on one of Ellen's ovaries, so he had called in an oncologist, and a medical team would have to operate immediately to remove the growth to see whether the cancer had spread. It would take several hours, he told me, so I might as well go take a walk and come back later.

Dizzy from the news, I drove to a friend's house for solace. No sooner had I sat down than a young Habad rabbi I knew happened by. I told him the news, and he instructed me to recite certain psalms while he went to the telephone to call the Lubavitcher Rebbe. It was comforting to focus my attention on the Hebrew verses. As I felt my world collapsing around me, I had to steel myself to recite those lines beginning with the letters that comprised Ellen's Hebrew name. I was doing *something* besides falling apart; the prayer was a way of fending off the consuming fear of profound loss.

Within moments, the Rebbe's personal secretary answered the phone. He was in the very same room with the revered spiritual leader and conveyed my distress to him. The Rebbe immediately began *davenen* for my wife. After a short time, he told his secretary to assure me that Ellen would be all right.

And she was. It took an agonizing week for all the tests to come in, but when they did, the doctors found no metastasis at all. They had discovered the usually fatal ovarian cancer so early that the prognosis was indeed excellent. Ellen had only half an ovary, but we were told that after she healed, we could again begin our attempts to achieve a pregnancy.

After a gut-wrenching year of mind-altering Clomid pills, injections of Perganol, and intimacy by the ovulation chart, I told Ellen I would follow her lead in pursuing adoption. I was done struggling. I had to give up my neatly planned schedule for making a family and simply surrender to whatever God had in mind for us. Ellen underwent another surgery as a precautionary measure to remove what remained of her second ovary. I have offered prayers of thanksgiving many, many times since, and now nearly twenty years later, there has been no trace of a recurrence.

What's more, adoption proved much easier than we had feared. We believe Hashem sent us a wonderful son, our Rafael, and we recently celebrated his bar-mitzvah. As we tell him, and as we ourselves have come to believe, all of the angst of a miscarriage, fertility treatments, and cancer, turned out to be well worth it, when the result was having him. After all, we tell him, if Hashem can implant a soul into a mother's womb the usual way, surely He is capable of sending the soul meant for us by this indirect path.

A Hebrew proverb says, *Gam zu le-tovah*, "This, too, is for the good." From our perspective after the fact, we can readily acknowledge that was the case through these traumatic experiences. We also know that the real spiritual task is to recognize *Gam zu le-tovah* from the outset, right when the undesirable event occurs. Not at all easy.

Terrorists, Again

"Introduction to Islam" was one of the courses I taught at Williams and was now teaching at USF. But by this time, there was a palpable change in the classroom. For one thing, at USF's more cosmopolitan campus, my students were more likely to be Palestinian or Syrian than Anglo. While they respected my "objectivity" in dealing with the subject, nevertheless I became more and more uncomfortable teaching Islam and resolved not to teach it again.

One of my best students was a very bright Palestinian woman, and I became friendly with her and her husband, a colleague in another college at USF. We had many conversations, polite enough but with a stressful undertone. Since I was also affiliated with the department of international studies, I became increasingly aware of an imbalance in its teaching about the Middle East. The department brought in Islamist speakers, one after another, and many of its public programs had a harshly anti-Israel tenor. All of this is no longer unusual on American college campuses, but that doesn't mean I especially liked it.

At one point, a proposal reached the chairman of our religious studies department for us to become involved in establishing an Islamic-oriented think tank. A leading member of the local Muslim community asked us to prepare a funding proposal for "one of the Saudi princes," so that we could house such a center. He told us to "think big." We came up with a proposal that amounted to several million dollars, but our friend scoffed, telling us that was not a big amount. Eventually, the figure of $30 million was bandied about, a staggering sum in the context of our university and our department. I became suspicious when we were told that the money had been granted. The speakers who had come to our campus had included Shaikh Omar Hassan al-Turabi, an Islamist leader in the Sudan. Polarizing public figures, such as Ramadan Abdullah Shallah, now secretary general of Palestinian Islamic Jihad in Damascus, joined USF's faculty to teach Arabic and Middle East studies. I went as far up as the university's president to express my alarm about what was going on, but no one likes a "nay-sayer," and the administration dismissed my suspicions and fears. For this and other reasons, I felt I ought to look for a less threatening academic environment.

The rest of the story is well known, at least in Florida. My student's husband is now awaiting trial for raising funds to support terrorism. He stands accused of funneling millions of dollars to the vilest of the Middle East's terrorists. The $30 million never materialized, and USF went through a period of being internationally reviled as "Jihad University of Florida." And despite all this, the faculty union still considers the school's entire horrific connection to terrorist funding to be just a matter of academic freedom.

Back to the Rebbe

For a few years, we were pleased with the Jewish life we had created for ourselves in Tampa. However, we began to feel pangs of dissatisfaction. Our Conservative Jewish observances of *kashrut*, ritual purity, Shabbat, and the holy days no longer felt high enough. Especially on Yom Kippur, I was struck by how painful the fast was for most of the synagogue's congregants, who stoically endured the long, long services and the hunger pangs. It seemed as if no one there felt any of the spiritual exhilaration that Ellen had experienced in the Cochin synagogue. In fact, for us, Yom Kippur with its promise of divine atonement was more of a deep renewal and a pleasure than an ordeal. Why did they do it, I wondered, why did they sit there hungry, when they seemed to get so little out of it?

Our limited Jewish knowledge also nagged at us, and made us feel we were stagnating. By this time, Ellen had become editor of the local Jewish newspaper, and I was, after all, a professor of religious studies. This meant that to everyone's mind, we were *hakhamim,* learned and wise. But we knew much better. When some friends decided to open a small Orthodox shul in our neighborhood, we chipped in, and we prayed there with increasing frequency. We did our best; our observance of the dietary laws increased, and our celebration of Shabbat became more and more intense. Every week on Shabbat, we filled our table with guests so that we could sing, and talk, and imbibe the holy spirit of Shabbat as much as possible. But we felt no choice but to drive to the synagogue, considered a desecration of the holy day. Essentially, we felt as if we had come as far as we could in Tampa.

I came to learn of an opening on the Asian religions faculty at Florida International University in Miami, and I applied for it. Uncharacteristically, I followed my application with phone calls to the head of the search committee, who confided that I was at the top of the list. I became hopeful. I knew that Miami was home to the third-largest Jewish community in North America, and I became enamored of the possibility of raising our level of knowledge and observance there. The fly in the ointment, the committee chair told me, was that I was a full professor and, therefore, commanded a relatively high salary on FIU's modest academic scale, and the dean would have to be convinced that I was worth the investment. After a very successful on-campus interview, I had to endure the wait. The dean was hedging, I learned, and my prospects were diminishing.

In desperation, I went to the Habad rabbi again and told him how much I wanted this job. When he asked me why, I told him that I wanted to improve my spiritual life. He faxed the Rebbe, and the very next day, I received a phone call from Miami.

The job was mine if I wanted it.

12

The Dalai Lama's "Jewish Secret"
Dharamsala

～

Just before being awarded the Nobel Prize in 1989, His Holiness, the fourteenth Dalai Lama of Tibet, briefly met with Jewish leaders at a Buddhist monastery in New Jersey.[1] As the spiritual and temporal leader of a people who had been conquered by Communist China fifty years ago, the world's preeminent Buddhist monk wanted to learn what he termed the "Jewish secret" of surviving exile. After all, he reasoned, the Jews had the experience: nineteen hundred years of living in the Diaspora, all the while preserving their distinct religion. Surely the Tibetan people could benefit from Jewish expertise.

The conversation resumed a year later. As a scholar of South Asian religions, including Tibetan Buddhism, and as a committed Jew, I was invited to join a delegation of eight rabbis and scholars to meet with the Dalai Lama and other Tibetan leaders. We met in Dharamsala, a hill station in the Himalayan foothills of northern India, seat of the Tibetan government-in-exile.

En Route: Reb Zalman

On my journey from Florida, I ran into Reb Zalman, a fellow delegate to Dharamsala, at JFK Airport. He had written a Hebrew benediction (*berakhah*) especially for the occasion, and he asked me to translate it into Tibetan. He explained that there are benedictions for meeting scholars and for meeting kings, but none for meeting someone who combines both roles. So he composed: "Blessed art Thou, L-rd our God, King of the universe, Who has imparted of Thy compassionate awareness unto those who honor and respect Thy Names."

---

[1] The chapter is based on Nathan Katz, "The Jewish Secret and the Dalai Lama," *Conservative Judaism* 43, no. 4 (Summer 1991): 33–46.

Driving to Dharamsala

We drove from Delhi to Dharamsala in a four-car convoy. I rode with Zalman and Rabbi Jonathan Omer-Man, a teacher of Jewish meditation in Los Angeles. It was quite an experience traveling through the tense Indian night with two mystics, and the conversation turned to theologies of exile.

I related an eighth-century Tibetan prophecy about the destruction of Buddhism in Tibet and its reestablishment in the "land of the red-faced people," taken to refer to the Americas. I explained that according to the law of karma, all of our actions in this world bear moral results, and that many Tibetans understand the loss of their homeland to be a consequence of their centuries of self-imposed isolation. When Tibet needed diplomatic friends, she had none. They also felt that their exile was made meaningful by the fact that the loss of Tibet had led directly to the spread of Buddhism to western countries. We wondered whether Tibetans also consider themselves "a light to the nations," an *or goyim*? Echoes of Isaiah.

Visualizations, Again

Jonathan was intrigued by the Tibetan Buddhist meditation practice known as "deity-yoga," wherein the practitioner visualizes an aspect of divinity, and then proceeds to identify with that mind-created deity. One attains enlightenment by practicing *as though one is already enlightened.* According to the Dalai Lama's Gelukpa branch of Tibetan Buddhism, this technique is the highest, most effective route to enlightenment. Jonathan and Zalman speculated about the anthropomorphism inherent in the exilic idea of the *galut ha-Shekhinah*, the exile of God's presence, and they compared it with deity-yoga visualizations.

We pondered the Dalai Lama's question about the "Jewish secret." Was our survival due to our democratized emphasis upon education as a goal for all Jews? Or to the development of vernacular languages, such as Yiddish or Judezmo? Or the genius of the rabbis in developing Halakhah? Or was it enforced from the outside by anti-Semitism and ghettoization? Most promising was the notion suggested by Rebbetzin Blu Greenberg, an Orthodox feminist leader and writer in New York, that the primacy of the home replaced the destroyed Temple in Jewish observance, and thus made Judaism more portable and especially equipped for survival in exile.

One idea was being overlooked, I offered: the belief that God's providence ensured Jewish survival. Whether it was God or the *belief in* God that sustained Judaism, I couldn't say. Zalman said there are two ways to ask why in

Hebrew: *maddu'a* and *lammah*, the former looking for etiology, for origins, and the latter for purposes, for teleology. Were we being asked *how* did we survive, or *why* did we survive? Understanding Jewish survival, he said, required a bifocal response, considering the interplay of causes and orientations.

Stymied on the Road

Late at night, as we neared the Punjabi capital of Chandigarh, we were stopped at a military roadblock. I joined our travel agent in discussions with the sergeant. He wanted us to return to Delhi, a six-hour drive back (with nine hours still ahead of us to our destination), because violence at that very spot, just hours earlier, had led to the imposition of a strict curfew. Even after reading the newspapers the next morning, it wasn't clear who had killed whom. Were high-caste Hindus rioting against a just-released government report that mandated stringent affirmative action quotas to benefit those from the lower castes? Or was it the controversy about the Muslim mosque constructed atop a Hindu temple at Ayodhya, birthplace of the warrior god Rama? Or was it the usual agitation for an independent Sikh homeland in the Punjab? How many people were killed? It was all very hazy, but we were able to persuade the sergeant to allow us to spend the night in a hotel in Chandigarh and proceed to Dharamsala at dawn the next day.

The next morning, we found the road to Dharamsala blocked by a student demonstration. We could not pass, so we hired one of the student leaders to guide us along the back roads, bypassing the disturbances. We managed to reach our destination, but immediately we began to worry about how we would get back to Delhi the next week.

A Plan of Action

Our schedule, prepared by the Dalai Lama's Council for Religious and Cultural Affairs, had us meeting not only with the Dalai Lama and his senior advisers, but also with the abbots of the major monasteries, with government officials, with youth leaders, and with western students of Buddhism, many of whom came from Jewish backgrounds. This well-conceived schedule would put us into contact with all strata of Tibetan leadership. That evening after dinner, we discussed the presentations we were preparing for our dialogue sessions with the Dalai Lama.

Marc F. Lieberman, a San Francisco ophthalmologist who had organized and raised funds for our delegation, asked each of us to share our hopes and apprehensions about the conversation. Blu Greenberg wanted to increase Tibetan friendship for Israel, and we carried with us an invitation for the Dalai Lama to visit there, which he did. Her apprehensions about the conference revolved around Jewish law. In our unusual setting, a Tibetan refugee community in India, was there a danger of contravening Halakhah? Prior to our arrival at the Dalai Lama's guesthouse, the kitchen had been scoured, burners lit, and cooking surfaces washed with boiling water. New pots, pans, plates, utensils, and cutlery had been purchased especially for us, and the food was to be strictly vegetarian. She and her husband, Rabbi Yitz Greenberg, an Orthodox leader and scholar from New York, inspected the kitchen and were satisfied with its *kashrut*. They were touched by the Tibetans' efforts, even though they remained a bit apprehensive.

Zalman hoped for further cooperation between the Tibetan and Jewish peoples, and was especially encouraged that we were to be in direct contact with several echelons of Tibetan leadership.

I voiced my sense of the deep responsibility we carried as "emissaries of the people," *shelihei ha-am*. As an academic, I am used to acting and speaking as an individual, but now I thought of myself as an emissary of the Jewish people to the Tibetan people. I agreed with Zalman that as historic and meaningful as this week was going to be, we had to look beyond our euphoria and find ways to institutionalize Tibetan-Jewish contacts. I pointed out that while numbers of Jews have studied Tibetan Buddhism, there were no Tibetans who had studied Judaism. I suggested that we raise funds to enable a Tibetan or two to pursue Jewish studies at the graduate level—perhaps one in Israel and one in America.

Professor Paul Mendes-Flohr of the Hebrew University in Jerusalem readily concurred with the need for academic exchanges. As a self-proclaimed secular Jew, he said he did not represent Jewish tradition but Jewish modernity. Surely no Jewish delegation could be complete without this perspective.

Rabbi Joy Levitt, who led a Reconstructionist synagogue on Long Island, had told her Sunday-school children about the dialogue and had asked them to prepare messages for the Dalai Lama. She showed us a notebook of touching letters and drawings with their heartfelt advice. One nine-year-old concisely wrote: "We Jews have always stuck together. No matter what. And if you Tibetans stick together, you will get your country back, too."

Rabbi Omer-Man, founder of the School for Jewish Meditation in Los Angeles, worried over the difficulty of discussing spirituality. He confessed that in many ways he had found it easier to discuss spirituality with Christians or Sufis than with fellow Jews. Happily, by the end of the week he came to revise that view.

Dr. Moshe Waldoks, a Massachusetts writer and scholar who since has become a congregational rabbi, had participated in the 1989 dialogue. He wondered whether this second meeting could possibly recapture the remarkable enthusiasm of the first.

Yitz Greenberg, a regular participant in interreligious dialogues, wanted to help the Tibetans by raising Jewish awareness about their persecution, possibly motivating American Jews to champion their cause in the U.S. Congress and at the United Nations. At that time, no American president had yet received the Dalai Lama, although President George W. Bush would do so in 2007, nor had he been invited to address Congress. The United Nations has been as silent about Tibet as it has been noisy about Israel.

Avodah Zarah Again

The discussion turned to how to address the Dalai Lama. Most westerners call him Your Holiness, but would that title imply that he is divine? Would expressing such an idea compromise an observant Jew? Would it be tantamount to idol worship, *avodah zarah*? Blu wanted to strike a balance between conveying the highest respect for the Dalai Lama and avoiding a theologically loaded form of address. New situations raise new problems, and we groped for ways to respond.

Speaking for Ourselves

We were invited to attend the inaugural session of the Himalayan Conference on the Five Traditional Sciences, being held at that time at the Dalai Lama's monastery, Thekchen Chöling. In his remarks before hundreds of Buddhist monks and scholars, the Dalai Lama lavishly praised Jews for "their courage and great determination" in preserving their religion and culture in the face of tremendous obstacles and sufferings. He said that Tibetans greatly admire Jews because "no matter how they are scattered through all corners of the earth, they maintained their sense of unity as a people," and he told the audience how lucky they were to have our delegation among them. His tremendous compliments brought tears to our eyes. One theme of the week began to emerge. By seeing ourselves reflected in the other, we form an image of who we are. In Christian and Muslim cultures, we Jews have seen condescension if not outright hostility in our reflections. But in Tibetan eyes, we saw reflected affection, respect, and even a bit of awe. How differently one knows oneself through such mirrors!

Listening to the Dalai Lama talk about us, I got the impression that he believed we Jews had survived by a collective act of will. I wondered. What preserved Judaism? Was it determination and courage, was it persecution, was it Hashem, or was it belief in Hashem? Is there a way to translate the idea of a transcendent justification for empirical reality into a Tibetan conceptual framework?

We had been invited to make a one-hour presentation to the Himalayan Conference, a unique opportunity to speak for ourselves before a distinguished group of Asian religious leaders. We delegated the responsibility to Yitz, and he and I worked together on the format of his talk. I suggested the traditional Tibetan way of analyzing a religion in terms of its view, its path, and its goal—*tawa, lam,* and *draybu.* Yitz liked the idea, and summarized the Jewish "view" as belief in a Creator God who endows creation with an inherent sanctity. The Jewish path, he said, involves the study of Torah, the performance of *avodah—* worship or ritual connections to the transcendent—and *hesed*—acts of loving-kindness, or our connections with one another. The Jewish goal is wholeness, or *shelemut,* the world-to-come, or *olam ha-ba,* and the divine-human partnership in the repair of the world, the Lurianic Kabbalistic idea of *tikkun ha-olam.*

Tibetan Buddhism maintains transformation as a central metaphor, in particular the transformation of the ordinary mind into the enlightened mind, or defilement into wisdom. Judaism, too, emphasizes transformation—the human-divine partnership in transforming this world into what it ought to be, *tikkun ha-olam.* We reflected on the interplay between the inner and outer complementary aspects of transformation. Yitz and I made a good team. His job as a rabbi was to teach about Judaism; mine as a scholar was to find appropriate metaphors to cross cultural boundaries. His talk was extremely well received.

Halakhah on the Road

Yitz and Zalman engaged in an animated discussion of what blessing to recite when they first met with the Dalai Lama. Zalman was ready with the new one he had composed for the occasion, but Yitz hesitated. We should not go about making up new liturgy, he cautioned. Joy agreed with Yitz; the occasion itself was sufficiently radical, there was no need to compose a new blessing. But which old blessing should we say? The liturgy offered one to use upon meeting a king, and another to say upon seeing a holy man, a *tzaddik.* Never before, as far as we knew, Zalman said, had there been an occasion for a Jew to recite a blessing upon meeting a wise man of another tradition who was also a head of state, and therefore we required a new blessing. Eventually, we reached a compromise: Zalman would recite the traditional blessing said upon meeting a king in Hebrew, followed by my Tibetan translation of the newly composed *berakhah*.

Then we hit another Halakhic conundrum. Zalman wanted to recite a *Mi she-berakh* blessing for the Dalai Lama and the Tibetan people, but he felt the traditional invocation for the blessing—"God of Abraham, God of Isaac, God of Jacob"—would be inappropriate. He asked me to identify three analogous Buddhist "patriarchs." Stretching a bit, I suggested the founder of the religion, the one who brought Buddhism to Tibet, and the founder of the Dalai Lama's Gelukpa sect of Buddhism. "*E-lokei Shakyamuni, E-lokei Padmasambhava, ve-lokei Tsong Khapa.*"

More discussions: In whose name should we make these blessings? "We are pioneering, we are trying to establish standards," Yitz said. Blu added, "We are entering into a new area, the sharing of rituals. And that is always more problematic than sharing thoughts and ideas." Indeed it was.

At the Palace

Finally, our meeting with the Dalai Lama in his fairly modest palace was to take place. As a professor of religious studies, part of my job is to meet religious leaders around the world, and I have been blessed to meet many— some saintly, most notably not. None, however, rises to the Dalai Lama's stature. His humor and warmth are striking, but it is his mind that impresses me the most. It goes beyond the usual sort of brilliance that one often encounters around universities. His mind penetrates with lightning rapidity; he gets to the heart of the matter more directly than anyone I have ever met. Perhaps it is the Buddhist teaching of non-egotism that creates such a flexible type of intelligence. Or perhaps he is just a remarkable man. Or both.

After Zalman's blessing, I was the first to speak. In my halting Tibetan, I greeted our hosts on behalf of the Jewish people. I experienced a rare moment of fulfillment; my years of study of Tibetan language and culture and my deep commitments to Judaism coalesced for a moment. The often disparate aspects of my life came together as the role of *sheli'ah ha-am* crystallized. The point of my remarks was that this Tibetan-Jewish dialogue was not really something new, for there are Sanskrit loan words in the Hebrew Bible, there have been contacts between India and Israel ever since the reign of King Solomon, similar legends are told about Solomon and the Buddha, the esoteric Tibetan system of Kalachakra Tantra ("cycles of time" teachings) and Jewish messianism may have a common source; and for millennia Jews have been intermediaries between India and the west.

Zalman then described Kabbalah and Jewish esotericism, the inner dimension of spirituality. His role in the dialogue was crucial. Tibetan Buddhism is a tradition especially rich in esotericism, and Tibetans would suspect that a religion not likewise esoteric might be superficial. Much of the overlap between our traditions lies in esotericism, and the Dalai Lama said that he found Judaism to be much more "sophisticated" than he had thought—in no small part in response to Zalman's animated descriptions of angels, of mysteries, of divine emanations, and of levels of being.

Next Yitz discussed how the rabbis expanded the scope of Jewish religious life and its conceptions of holiness in response to exile and the loss of the Temple. He was an excellent balance to Zalman's esotericism. He never failed to remind the Dalai Lama, and the rest of us, that while mysticism is indeed a revered part of Jewish tradition, it most definitely is "a minority opinion."

As Yitz described the Jewish observance of Shabbat, the Dalai Lama offered a most insightful comment. Yitz said that Shabbat harkens back to creation at the same time that it anticipates the messianic completion of the world. Jews live Shabbat as though the world were redeemed. The Dalai Lama drew upon his own meditational tradition of deity-yoga visualization to comment, "You mean that Shabbat is your people's visualization exercise?" How right on target! That is precisely what we do: through living "as if," we participate in the cosmic drama of redemption. An insight worthy of a Heschel!

Paul's secularism complemented Yitz's Orthodoxy. The Dalai Lama was intrigued that the family of Judaism is able to embrace both secular and religious members. Paul eloquently articulated the dilemma of modernity: personal fulfillment is the watchword of the modern world, whereas communal responsibility is the hallmark of tradition. We Jews are perceived as the first people to find a balance between the two—individualism and community—providing a model for any traditional people confronting the modern world.

The Jewish Home Away from Home

Fifteen years prior to the dialogue, when I was conducting my dissertation research at the Tibetan Library in Dharamsala, I came to know Alexander Berzin, a Harvard Ph.D. in oriental studies, who often served as the Dalai Lama's interpreter. Of Jewish background, Alex had become an esteemed teacher of Buddhism. Observing him during the dialogue, I could not help but wonder what he was thinking, what sparks within his Jewish soul were being ignited. After the preliminary sessions, Alex said to me with a sense of urgency: "You've got to tell them more about the home. They don't understand about how the home can be a vehicle for religious transmission. Unless you teach them about how to observe religion in the home, the Tibetans will not be able to preserve their traditions."

Perhaps more than any other people, Tibetans know about the transformation of the mind, but they do not know so well how to transform *this* reality, a process we Jews call the sanctification of the everyday. While we can and should learn from them about the former, they need to learn from us about the latter.

Along these lines, Zalman had the idea to conduct a "Seder workshop" to show the Tibetans how a parallel to the Seder meal could be developed around the life of the Buddha. The purpose would be to show the Tibetans a way of adapting their traditions to a home transmission. We didn't manage to do it, but the idea was on target, according to Alex—who ought to know.

Tea and Conversion

Over lunch with Zalman and a Buddhist monk named George Chernoff, we heard a story about the late revered Tibetan teacher, Lama Thubten Yeshe. Lama Yeshe had many Jewish students, of course, and he often said, "If what they learn from me helps to make them better Jews, then I am most happy; then I will have served my purpose as a religious teacher." I am reminded of how Trungpa Rinpoche, the controversial Tibetan master, admonished me several times to observe Shabbat. Tibetans don't seek converts; religion for them is not a banner or an allegiance, but a way of improving people, calming the mind, and cultivating altruism. I cannot help but think that if the spiritual traditions of Judaism were somehow more accessible, many fewer young Jews would seek spiritual edification elsewhere.

Shabbat in the Himalayas

That afternoon we had a rather formal dialogue with the abbots of Tibet's leading monasteries, which have been rebuilt in exile in India. After the formal session, we invited them back to our guesthouse for Kabbalat Shabbat and dinner. It was remarkable to be greeted with a broad smile and a softly spoken "Shabbat Shalom" by someone wearing a maroon monk's robe.

Our haste to get back to the guesthouse in time for Shabbat led to a humorous miscommunication. When our hosts heard of our anxiety to get back before sunset, and came to understand that this haste was for some inscrutable religious reason, they concluded that we must be sun worshippers, needing to worship our God as the sun set. Apparently, Tibetans don't think very highly of sun worshippers, and it took more conversation to sort out that the sun merely marked the time for us and was not the object of our veneration. Our lama hosts seemed pleased to be reassured that we were not "mere" primitives.

Each morning we *davened* the *Shaharit* prayers outside our guesthouse, overlooking the beautiful Kangra Valley, with the snow-capped Himalayas to our left, eagles soaring overhead. I had never so deeply enjoyed *davenen* than with this remarkable group in this remarkable place under these remarkable circumstances. People took turns as *baalei-tefillah*, leading the prayers, and I led *Shaharit* for Shabbat morning. What *chutzpah!* Among these learned rabbis, creative liturgists, and scholars, I led with my highly amateurish—but sincere—*chazzanut* (cantorial chanting)!

After prayers, we held an open house for western students of Buddhism, many of them monks or nuns, many Jewish. It was an occasion for stimulating dialogues. One nun of Jewish origin, Thubten Chödron, sought to understand Judaism by examining me in the rapid-fire, dialectical style of Buddhist monastic training. I thoroughly enjoyed the exchange. She asked how I would explain that Judaism is not just a set of beliefs and doctrines, but actually a path, a way to practice. These were questions I could answer. Finally, she turned to the God idea, asking how I could justify belief in an omniscient, omnipotent God, given the pervasiveness of suffering in a world created by that God. Of course, I could not answer that universal question, but I assured her that my inability to do so did not diminish either my ability to participate in Judaic religious life or my access to the inner, experiential dimensions of our tradition. I doubted that she was intellectually satisfied with my answers, but, then again, neither am I. Her highly intelligent questions helped clarify my beliefs.

That afternoon we met with a group of "young, educated Tibetans." They were secularists; some advocated armed opposition to the Chinese occupation of their country, in contradiction to the Dalai Lama's insistence upon nonviolence. They were especially interested in one particular Jewish institution, youth camps such as Ramah. Paul had spoken about his formative experiences at Camp Ramah, how it instilled a sense of solidarity with his people at an impressionable age. After further discussions, we decided to invite a Tibetan to observe our summer youth camps to determine how they could be adapted to the circumstances of exiled Tibetans. This project went well, and now similar Tibetan summer youth camps are scattered around India.

Amid our engrossing conversations at Dharamsala, the members of our delegation were still concerned about how we could travel back to Delhi the next week. From what we could gather, the political situation had been deteriorating. The organizers of the delegation were trying to charter a small airplane to get us back, because the roads might not be safe.

Refugee Education

One evening, we visited the Tibetan Children's Village. More than half of its population comes from Tibet proper. Even many years after the occupation, mothers still make the dangerous, arduous journey across the Himalayas to deposit their children at the village to be raised in Tibet's cultural and religious traditions, a type of education that the Chinese rulers of Tibet still forbid. A mother who leaves her children is well aware of the likelihood that she may never see them again, since she must return home lest her family in Tibet suffer at the hands of their rulers. But she accepts the sacrifice in order to have her children raised to be proud of, and educated about, their Tibetan heritage.

A very typical encounter: Seeing my *kippah* (skullcap), a government official who was an Indian delegate to the Himalayan Conference, asked me, "Excuse me, sir, are you from Israel?" I replied that I was not, but that I was a member of the Jewish delegation. "I want to learn something about your people," he said. "All we read in the newspapers is very slanted. Can you recommend an authentic book I could read?" His attitude is typical of many, many Buddhists and Hindus throughout Asia. Their minds are open; we need only present our case intelligently, and it will be received. To build on that opportunity, we need to circumvent governments, and make direct contact with intellectuals and religious leaders.

Happily, in 2004, I was able to do exactly that. I gave a series of lectures and interviews on Indo-Judaic studies to newspapers and television programs. One interview aired in ten-minute segments for five consecutive nights on Doordarshan, the national government television network. I was told that the average nightly viewership was 230 million!

Meeting the Oracle

Another day of the conference started with a visit to Nechung Monastery, home of the State Oracle of Tibet. The medium for the Oracle, who was an unassuming Buddhist monk, described his experiences as a medium. Zalman compared notes, telling him about the prophets of ancient Israel, the visions in the Book of Daniel, and the mystical breastplates of the *kohen gadol*. The monk's descriptions of his sources and roots as a medium were remarkably similar to Biblical techniques for prophecy.

Our hosts understood our safety concerns about our return trip to New Delhi, and they kindly presented each of us with colored grains of rice known as *chené*. The colored rice, properly blessed and offered, is thought to be a powerful talisman against the dangers of the road. Tibetan travelers prize it, but as Yitz and I walked away from Nechung, *chené* in our hands, I asked him, "Rabbi, are we allowed to even have this stuff?" He replied that it was a sort of paradox. "If," he explained, "we have accepted this *chené* in the spirit of friendship and no more than that, then there is no violation of law. If, on the other hand, we think this might actually protect us, then there is a serious problem of idolatry, and, of course, it would be ineffective." Yitz's blue eyes twinkled. "Of course," he concluded, "if we accept it in the spirit of friendship, then it just might work!"

Back to the Palace

During the afternoon of our second and concluding session with the Dalai Lama, he answered a question from Shoshana Edelberg, a reporter for National Public Radio. She asked why he had invited Jews for such intensive dialogue. Without missing a beat, he replied: "I think we are both chosen people! We don't have exactly the same ideas, but we Tibetans believe we are chosen by Avalokiteshvara [the embodiment of Buddhist compassion and the protector deity of Tibet]. You believe you are chosen by the Creator God. So it is almost the same idea. Another reason: when we became refugees, we knew that our struggle would not be easy. It will take a long time, generations. Very often we would refer to the Jewish people, how they kept their identity and faith despite such hardship and so much suffering. And when external conditions were ripe, they were ready to rebuild their nation. So you see, there are many things to learn from our Jewish brothers and sisters."

Jonathan described Jewish systems of meditation, many of which have close parallels in Tibetan tradition. He told about the strained relations between the exoteric and esoteric wings of Judaism. He explained that most leaders want to bar all but the most observant from Judaism's mysteries, but that some do want to "open all the doors" to the esoteric. He said he preferred a bit more caution.

The following Shabbat, when I spoke about our dialogue in the New Delhi synagogue, the Jews there were amazed to hear that Jewish meditation exists. They did not know there was such a thing! It is very sad that most Jews know so little about Jewish meditation and spirituality. Clearly, we need to open our doors more widely if we are to keep our spiritual seekers inside our fold.

Moshe presented the Dalai Lama with a replica Torah scroll that Paul had brought from Israel. He described the four traditional levels of textual interpretation: the literal meaning, the "hinted-at" meaning, the "searched-for" meaning, and finally the esoteric meaning. The relation of commentary to text, and the mediation of the text by the tradition, are areas of close overlap between the Tibetan and Jewish traditions.

Blu then told the Dalai Lama about the Jewish home, the unique forms of observance and transmission reserved for the family. Perhaps this was the most fruitful of all our exchanges, especially from a Tibetan point of view. The Dalai Lama's fascination with our home-centered observances made me appreciate the singularity of Jewish traditions.

Finally, Joy spoke about Jewish communal institutions—the synagogue foremost, but also federations, Zionist alliances, religious schools, and burial societies. Clearly, the Tibetans were intrigued by the implications for organizing their own community, especially since theirs is even more attenuated than our own. She also presented the Dalai Lama with the notebook of letters and drawings from the children of her synagogue, and he read several of them. It was a touching moment, an especially deep level of human contact.

My Disharmonious Non-Question

After the presentations, I raised a difficult issue with the Dalai Lama, that of Jews who join other religions, including Tibetan Buddhism. "Your Holiness," I said, "I must speak with candor. There remains one issue that pains us. You have seen our deep sense of family. It is very painful to us, therefore, when one of our family chooses to leave us. On one hand, it is clear that Jewish people who adopt the Tibetan path benefit greatly as individuals. On the other hand, we suffer from a brain drain on a community level. Many of our finest, most intelligent, most spiritually inclined people are leaving us. I am not asking you a question, nor am I requesting you to make a statement. But on behalf of my coreligionists, I must tell you frankly how we feel."

The Dalai Lama was taken aback somewhat by my comment. He told us that Buddhism does not seek converts, but at the same time it makes no distinction among peoples. Anyone who wants to share the teachings of the Buddha is entitled to them; religion knows no national boundary. He explained further the Buddhist belief that the Buddha offered differing teachings to students of differing personalities; therefore, no one religious doctrine could satisfy everyone. His advice, however, was both understanding and sage: If you want to keep your people in your religion, then you must open your doors to spirituality. If you have esoteric traditions to offer, then they will not want to leave to seek them elsewhere.

"As a result of our meeting," he continued, "to speak quite frankly, I developed much more respect for Judaism because I found there a high level of sophistication. I think it is very important that you make these teachings available for everyone, especially intellectual people. Sometimes there is a danger to too much secrecy. Often qualified people are excluded from the practice, so I think the best thing is to be flexible. I have seen many similarities between your tradition and ours. If you make these teachings available, why would your people want Buddhist Tantra? You have your own Tantra! Many of your people have keen intelligence and very creative minds, and if they are not personally satisfied with what you offer them, then nobody could stop them from leaving and taking a new religion. Provide them with all the materials, all spiritual teachings. If you have these spiritual values, then there is no reason to fear; if you have no such values, then there is no reason to hold on. If you cannot provide spiritual satisfaction to others and at the same time insist on holding on to them, then that is foolishness. This is reality." He was entirely right, of course.

In the Shadow of the Shoah

At one point, the Dalai Lama revisited this theme. "Why is it so difficult for you to learn Jewish esoteric teachings? Why won't your teachers make them available to sincere, intellectual people?" Moshe Waldoks replied. "Now we must speak about the Holocaust. During this period, one-third of our people were exterminated. Among them, more than 80 percent of our rabbis and teachers were murdered. Our esoteric teachings died in Hitler's ovens, too." Unblinking, the Dalai Lama joined us in peering into the abyss. It was a wordless moment of deep empathy and understanding.

I came back to Dharamsala years later, escorting a group of FIU students. On that trip, we visited the tasteful "Museum of the Tibetan Holocaust," a Yad Yashem–inspired memorial to Tibetan suffering under the Chinese occupation. Talking with the curator, I was told that Israeli travelers had implored the

Jerusalem memorial's staff to visit Dharamsala to see the crude photographic exhibition that was the best the Tibetans could do at the time. The Israeli memorialists pitched in, resulting in a moving, tasteful, and sophisticated documentation of humanity's ongoing inhumanity.

Meanwhile, our session with the Dalai Lama concluded with Joy's beautiful chanting of *Kaddish de-Rabbanan*, the Jewish prayer for scholars, to which the lamas responded by "dedicating the merit" of the prayer to the welfare of all sentient beings—a Tibetan amen. We tearfully took leave of the Dalai Lama and his entourage, ennobled by the encounter and stirred by his challenge to open our doors wide.

Yitz summed things up in his own way: "As a result of exile, the Dalai Lama went from being a god to being a man. And he has grown enormously in the process." Alex thanked us for "making me proud to be a Jew." The nun Thubten Chodron also saw us off, presenting us with small gifts. After dinner, we loaded our luggage and newly purchased Tibetan carpets into our cars for the fifteen-hour overnight drive back to New Delhi. The State Oracle had assured us that we would be safe, so we departed somewhat relieved. We were grateful that our only obstacles on the road were mechanical.

With Sufis and Swamis in Delhi

On the delegation's last day in India, I took Blu, Zalman, and the poet Rodger Kamenetz on a whirlwind tour of some of Delhi's religious centers. I focused on living shrines, not ancient monuments, however beautiful. First was a Sufi shrine in an old Muslim section of town. To get there, we had to negotiate narrow alleys filled with leprous beggars and aggressive hawkers—in a sense, the stereotypically worst of India. I hated to bring Blu here; she is such an *eshet hayil* (virtuous woman) that seeing such poverty upset her visibly. At the same time, I respected her *sekhel* (intelligence) so much that I wanted to show her what was real, unvarnished, beggars and all. From there Zalman led us to the shrine of Hazrat Inayat Khan, a modern Sufi saint who brought his esoteric tradition to the west. Then we visited the new Baha'i temple—an imposing sculpture, but somehow cold in spirit. Another cab ride took us to the tomb of Sa'id Sarmad, the eclectic Jewish Sufi-Yogi of Mughal India. Keeping the ritually prescribed distance, Zalman and I recited *Kaddish* for him. After that, it was Sikh *gurudwara*, Jaina temple, Buddhist monastery, and Hindu temple. The day was as uplifting as it was exhausting; we were in India, after all.

Who should we run into in our hotel but Ram Dass, the Jewish-born Richard Alpert, a Harvard professor who was fired for LSD research; he was now a Hindu guru! Ram Dass was a longtime associate of Zalman, and he joined us in our visit to New Delhi's synagogue, Judah Hyam Prayer Hall. I think he made the tenth for our *minyan*. It was time for evening prayers, known as *Arbith* in the Sephardi world. At my insistence and in deference to local custom, we used the Sephardic prayerbook. Yitz led the prayers so beautifully that we didn't want to stop praying. We lingered over one additional psalm after another, a spiritual farewell to India.

Our delegation met my old friend Ezekiel Isaac Malekar, *shammash* (caretaker) and lay *chazzan* of the small synagogue, Judaism's flickering light in India's capital. Only about a half dozen Jewish families remain in Delhi, but with the addition of diplomats and tourists, the synagogue usually musters a *minyan* on Friday evenings (Saturday is a working day in India) and holidays. Ezekiel is a small, dynamic man who represents Judaism at most ecumenical events. He knows the local Tibetan lamas, Sufis, Sikh leaders, and swamis, and evidently relishes his interfaith role.

Ram Dass joined us for dinner at a strictly vegetarian Hindu restaurant; I vouched for its *kashrut* to Yitz and Blu. Ram Dass told us that he divided his time between retreats in the Himalayas and fundraising for his Seva Foundation, which helps maintain hospitals in India. He looked very well after the years, although he has been infirm of late, and he discussed meditation with Jonathan, commenting that he would like to refer straying Jews back into the fold via Jonathan's meditation school in Los Angeles. I was struck by the irony: probably few people in the world had led more Jews away from Judaism than Ram Dass, yet now he wanted to find avenues to lead some back. I was also struck by how pitiably small his knowledge of Judaism was. After eating, we chanted grace, *Birkat ha-Mazon*. Ram Dass leaned across the table and asked me: "That was a very pretty tune you sang after the meal. What was that?" With such a paltry background, no wonder he left!

Thoughts from India

Everyone else had left, but I stayed in New Delhi for a few more days, intending to meet with leaders of the city's Tibetan and Jewish communities to report on our dialogue—as well as to do some shopping! The hiatus also gave me some time to think about those two remarkable weeks.

For an observant Jew, participation in this sort of dialogue raises issues of *avodah zarah*, a derogatory term meaning "other people's worship," something to be avoided at all costs by observant Jews. Is Tibetan Buddhism *avodah zarah*, or is it another name of God? Blu said that when she told her father where she was going on this trip, he was even more upset than when she had supported women's ordination, and he began studying the Talmud's tractate on *avodah zarah*. What is relatively easy for modern secularists is fraught with difficulties for someone traditionally religious. Yet, the question is not simple. Ample halakhic authorities, from Sa'adia Gaon to Maimonides, sometimes held accommodating views regarding other religions. Somehow this liberal thread has receded into the background, and more rigid views have come to the fore. The texts do not hold a monolithic view, so Yitz and Blu were struggling to uphold a perspective that was simultaneously Orthodox and open to otherness, to the modern world.

Our delegation contained some remarkable individuals, and we blended into a strong team. I admired what Yitz was trying to do within the Jewish world as founding president of CLAL, The National Jewish Center for Learning and Leadership. I saw him as a human stitch straining to close the fissures in the fabric of the Jewish people. He was trying to hold together Orthodox and non-Orthodox Jews by nurturing and maintaining a respectful dialogue between them. Zalman, in his way, was also trying to hold Jews together—Jews (like what Ellen and I once were) who might otherwise leave the family for what they perceive to be more fertile spiritual soil. Each man had made many enemies for his efforts. I felt deep solidarity with both of them.

I admired the Dalai Lama even more than I had before. He uniquely inspires others. Even before our first dialogue session, somehow all of us knew we would have to rise to the occasion spiritually. Through our prayers, through the rarefied environment of Dharamsala, through the inspiration of all those whom we represented, we were able to do so. We were able to approach his level, and I think it was the highest any of us had ever attained.

Coming out of this dialogue, we all learned something about the Tibetan people, their remarkable culture, and their heroic efforts to maintain that culture in exile. More important, however, is that we had all come to know ourselves differently. Of course, we learned a great deal from the other Jewish delegates in this notably learned and articulate group. Deeper than that, we had seen ourselves reflected by a new other—a Tibetan other, an other that knew us in respect and affection. Having seen this reflection, perhaps we could generate those feelings toward ourselves.

I felt opened spiritually and emotionally as well as intellectually. The dialogue had been so much of the heart. Each session had opened and concluded with expressions of mutual affection.

We Jews have always felt that we are a "light to the nations," that we have something valuable to offer the world. How marvelous it had been to meet eager recipients of our message, recipients who had much to teach us, and how singularly rare! Dialogue, it is said, transforms both participants; and so this one did.

13

A Black Hat Affair
New York

∼

The image of twenty thousand Orthodox Jews in a basketball arena sounds more like the punch line to a Catskills joke than anything else, but on March 1, 2005, it really took place—twice, in fact, at Madison Square Garden in Manhattan and simultaneously at Continental Airlines Arena in the Meadowlands, New Jersey.

The occasion was the eleventh "Completion of Learning the Talmud One Page per Day," or *Siyum ha-Shas Daf Yomi*. In 1923 a Polish rabbi came up with a revolutionary approach to studying the Talmud, the *sine qua non* of traditional Jewish scholarship. His page-a-day innovation had Jews all over the world learning the same page at the same time. Not only did this technique create a sense of unity, *ahdut*, but it meant that a traveling Jew could pick up his studies exactly where he left off, whether he was in New York, Melbourne, Paris, or Tel Aviv. By routinizing learning, he created an inviting open door that many thousands of people used to enter the world of traditional scholarship, although the torrid pace made the exercise more like reading an index to a book than the book itself. Even at such breakneck speed, daily learners needed seven and a half years to get through the whole Talmud.

My mother passed away eight years before this grand event. One traditional way of expressing respect for a departed parent—indeed, for coping with the grief—is to learn in her or his memory. Since the new *daf yomi* cycle was just beginning, I decided to undertake the Talmud's first tractate, *Massekhet Berakhot*, on the subject of blessings. Classes were at six in the morning in my little Miami Beach shul. I was going to morning prayers each day anyway, to recite the memorial prayer known as *Kaddish* for my mother, so I decided to rise an hour earlier for the task of learning the Talmud.

On particularly somber days, such as the fast of the Ninth of Av, a date when calamity after calamity befell the Jewish people, you are not allowed to learn because learning is considered to be such a pleasure that it is incompat-

117

ible with the sadness of the day. I never before had a real sense of learning as a pleasure, even though I had spent many years in universities. But after a few months of *daf yomi*, learning with Rabbi Moti Shifman, I was hooked. For seven and a half years, I got to shul at six most mornings, struggling with the Aramaic language of the Talmud, straining my mind to follow its complex logic.

Learning Talmud, Cheering Dr. J.

About sixty thousand people in and around New York City, plus that number again all around the world, were joined together through satellite hookups, and gathered that afternoon in time for evening prayers. I was stirred to hear so many people enthusiastically respond to the prayer leader, their voices resonating in a huge hall that was more accustomed to cries of "DEE-FENSE, DEE-FENSE" than "*YEHE SHEMEH RABBA MEVARAKH.*" I glanced around the building, home court of the New Jersey Nets. As a Philadelphia-raised NBA fan, I could barely suppress my laughter when I saw the banner commemorating the high-flying grace of Julius Erving, one of my favorite players. How appropriate, I thought, that this homecoming brought me both to the source of my faith and to the echo of one of Dr. J's tomahawk dunks.

To the outsider, a group of Orthodox Jews looks uniform. Indeed, we looked the same in our black suits and hats and white shirts. But to the insider, the diversity was inspiring. The congregation included Modern Orthodox Jews with their knitted yarmulkes (*kippot serugot*); Lubavitch Hasidim sporting fedoras with turned-down brims; Yemenites with long, curled sidelocks; Hungarian Hasidim wearing a bewildering array of fur hats known as *shtraymlech*, whose shape and precise type of fur immediately informed the cognoscenti of their precise lineage; Lithuanian yeshiva students sporting upturned black hats worn toward the back of the head; as well as the occasional nonconformist in a white *kippah* and perhaps a pale blue shirt. As is often said in the Orthodox world, there are many shades of black.

The *siyum* (completion celebration) consisted of speech after speech, mostly in English but a good number in Yiddish too, and an occasional talk in Hebrew. Most of the men present had no difficulty moving between the three languages. "Look around you, look around you, my brothers," exclaimed one rabbi, a Holocaust survivor like many of those present. "Who could have imagined that not only would we survive, but now, sixty years later, we are stronger than ever. More people are learning than ever have. More people have completed *Shas* [i.e., the Talmud] during this seven-and-a-half year cycle than ever have before." Our resolute actions represented divine stubbornness; we adamantly refused to concede that the past was over and done.

Niggunim, wordless melodies, punctuated the speeches. These tunes are the staple of Hasidism, a movement designed to open spirituality to those who lack extensive background or the linguistic and analytical skills required for deep scholarship. The high point was the recitation of the *Hadran,* the "I shall return to you" prayer that Jews intone when completing any section of the Talmud. "I will return to you, dear tractate on blessings, I will return to you." This time, this loving prayer embraced not just one text, but the entire Talmud. Before the *Hadran,* the crowd heard the last verses of the tractate on impurity (*Massekhet Niddah*). The first sentences of the tractate on blessings followed the prayer, thus framing a moment in a never-ending cycle instead of a linear completion and recommencement. A *niggun* followed the tearful, passionate *Hadran,* and all twenty thousand rose in an instant and began clapping, singing, and dancing as best we could in the narrow aisles among the steeply tiered rows of seats. The revelry, laughter, and tears, the awe at what we had accomplished and the joy of our neighbors' accomplishments, commingled with the loss of the old world and the thrill of the new.

A Learning Lifestyle

Learning Talmud each morning was at times uplifting, at times disconcerting, at times boring, and at times simply inconvenient. Tracking an argument through its subtle textures, or coming to appreciate an especially uplifting insight, or successfully wrestling with the Talmud's half-Hebrew, half-Aramaic syntax—these were moments to relish. On the other hand, some of the things the text says about women, or about non-Jews, or about ordinary people (*ammei ha-aretz*) fly in the face of many of the values I hold dear. The text has an undeniable arrogance, a chauvinism. Staring at the Talmud's stark, oversized pages each dawn, I tried to kick my brain into gear, but as often as not I succumbed to drowsy, early morning reveries. And there was the plain logistical bother: I left my long-suffering wife alone to get our son ready for school; I needed special strategies to get to the office (three-quarters of an hour of heavy traffic away) early enough; and I had to put off necessary household errands and tasks.

The page-a-day methodology of *daf yomi* means that one speeds through it rather than delving into the text's deeper meanings. Undoubtedly, though, even a cursory familiarity with the Talmud, also known as the Oral Torah, en-

ables one to begin to follow the more philosophical readings. The Talmud is
the indispensable foundation of Jewish scholarship.

As I write this on a Sunday in Jerusalem, I smile to think that the discourses I heard yesterday from two of contemporary Judaism's leading
thinkers—one by Rabbi Adin Steinsaltz during morning prayers at the Habad
Synagogue in the Old City, and one by Rabbi Shlomo Riskin after the conclusion of Shabbat at the central Modern Orthodox synagogue—would have
been utterly incomprehensible to me without my cursory, or *peshat*, familiarity with the texts they repeatedly cited. Traditional Jewish intellectual life, like
Jewish spirituality, is opaque without a firm grounding in its textual sources,
and that is both the strength and the weakness of the tradition.

Despite these downs and ups, learning Talmud has been one of the richest spiritual endeavors of my life . . . and not just because I managed to get
through it all. There is the discipline, of course, of a strict daily routine. There
is a kind of satisfaction bordering on smugness about having done so much—
swimming half a mile, learning for an hour, praying—before the work day
began. And there is the inspiration of doing it with my *daf* buddies. Even as I
sometimes struggled to get to shul so early, seeing my fellow learners—physi-
cians, attorneys, shopkeepers, teachers, businessmen—gave me not only camaraderie, but a real sense of what is important. And that is learning, the
prerequisite for full participation in traditional Jewish life. Learning is dedi-
cation to God, expressed in the tradition's highest terms.

14

Life as a Mindful OJ
Jerusalem and Miami Beach

~

When we first moved to Miami Beach and I began to meet the men who attend its synagogues, I was struck by several things. First, my profession was perhaps the fourth or fifth thing people wanted to know about me; it just wasn't so much a priority. In the secular world, profession comes first, but in this religious demimonde, learning, piety, and ritual performance matter more. As I was reciting the memorial prayer for my mother at that time, leading the prayers became one of the key ways I had available to me to express my respect for her, or to elevate her soul in heaven, as the tradition puts it.

Was that ever intimidating! In Orthodox synagogues, nobody hesitates to correct any mistakes you might make while leading the *davenen* (praying) or reading from the Torah. Given that I made a lot of mistakes, especially at first, my friends rebuked me publicly more often than I care to remember. Accepting a rebuke as a kindness became an ego-taming exercise for me. At the beginning, I was drenched in nervous sweat by the time I removed my *tallit* (prayer shawl) after prayers. Gradually overcoming my shortcomings became exhilarating.

Whether saying morning prayers in shul, or rising at 4:00 a.m. for meditation at a Buddhist monastery, some such routine is essential for spiritual growth. Any genuine tradition places great demands on its practitioners, demands that they must welcome as opportunities for growth. In an effort to increase their membership rosters, and to make religion "relevant" and "accessible," some religious leaders have systematically weakened this sense of demand. The concept of obligation (*hiyuv*) has been replaced with a panacea of personal growth. Not God, not the Dharma, not tradition and family, but personal feelings have become the standard by which religion is judged and marketed. In my opinion, that is where traditional spirituality and its contemporary version part ways.

Kabbalah and Pornography

Not long ago, I had the delight of spending the better part of a day with Adin Steinsaltz, one the most eminent rabbis of our era, a Talmud scholar and Kabbalist, and also one of the finest intellects I have ever engaged. I asked the rabbi what he thought of today's pervasive pop-Kabbalah, and about contemporary American spirituality in general. What he said at first alarmed me, but upon reflection, the depth of his thinking became apparent.

He told me that the Kabbalah Centers are to genuine Kabbalah what pornography is to love. Popular spirituality is not only a dilution, I inferred from his analogy, but a perversion of the real thing.

Pornography, Rabbi Steinsaltz taught me, is about your own sensations, however pleasurable, and not about the other. It has no sense of *hiyuv*, no obligation, nothing which binds us to the other, who becomes a mere object. It is all about the self, so much so that the other is lost in superficiality. Love, on the other hand, is entirely about the other. It intrinsically contains caring and obligation. In other words, it has depth. Both pornography and love involve the erotic, of course, but an eroticism that is utterly self-referential is a pale shadow of an eroticism rooted in love.[1]

Searching for Depth

Whatever else it may be, Orthodox living is deep. It resonates historically as it resonates psychologically and spiritually. Not so long after I adopted the routine of going to the morning *minyan*, I visited the Shrine of the Book, which is attached to the Israel Museum in Jerusalem. The "book" enshrined there is commonly referred to as the Dead Sea Scrolls, collection of 2,000 year old holy scrolls from the ancient community of Qumran, in the Judean Hills to the south of Jerusalem.

Some of the scrolls are idiosyncratic to the sect that inhabited Qumran's caves, and others – such as the Isaiah scroll – are also found in the Torah. The museum displays a set of *tefillin* (called in English by the Greek term, *phylacteries*, which seems to be no more accessible than the Hebrew word) that is more than 2,000 years old. I was transfixed by it. Each morning I don a nearly identical set, wrapping its straps around my left arm and the top of my head. The conjunction of my own daily practice with a 2,000-year-old museum piece struck me viscerally. How ancient, how wise, how profound. I felt my-

---

[1] Nathan Katz, "Angel & Ape—Revered Religious Authority Rabbi Adin Steinsaltz Discusses the Material, the Spiritual, and the Divine," *Loft* (Miami, March 2005), pp. 50–53.

self not as an individual isolated in time, but as part of a very old tradition. I felt as though I just as well might take the Qumran *tefillin* out of the museum display, wrap them around my head and arm, and pray. Contemporary and antique, a reflection of the depth in which I had begun to immerse myself. My body shook, my hair felt as if it stood on end as such thoughts raced through my mind.

Some time later, I visited a special exhibit at the Smithsonian Institution in Washington. The centerpiece was a finial from the Temple of Solomon, said to be the only relic from the *Bayit ha-Rishon*, the First Temple, approximately three thousand years old. It was made of ivory carved in the shape of a pomegranate and was used solely by my priestly ancestors, the *kohanim*. My attention was drawn to the single word carved onto it: *Kadosh*, holy. What struck me was the ease with which I, or anyone who could read even a minimum of Hebrew, could decipher the ancient letters. I wondered whether any other language exists whose ciphers were readily discernable after so long an interval. Continuity. Living history. Again, depth. The fact that recent investigations have shown, alas, that the finial was a fraud only slightly diminishes my sense of awe, which in memory focuses on the experience, not the carving.

Jewish Meditation

In an important sense, meditation is meditation. Once you have mastered one technique, learning more methods is relatively simple. So my years of practicing yoga or Buddhist meditations made the crossover to Jewish meditation all the easier. Some of the techniques are so very similar. Mentally repeating sacred words, perhaps the *Shema* or a phrase from Psalms, is technically no different from Hindu *mantra* repetition or Sufi *dhikr* practice. As a matter of fact, in Jewish mysticism, the phrase you hold as you meditate is called by the same name, *dekhir*. A Kabbalistic meditation that takes the Shabbat candles as a focal point is not unlike the Buddhist use of the *kasina*, or object of meditation. You direct your consciousness into, out of, and around different points of the selected object.

Judaism's various guided meditations are much like Tantric visualizations, as conveyed through the relevant *sadhana* texts. The self-reflection (*heshbon ha-nefesh*) described by one of my favorite Jewish mystics, Rabbi Hayyim Moses Luzzatto of Venice, recalls the way I learned to apply Buddhist mindfulness to memory. The quiet hour spent before morning prayers described in the tractate on blessings of the Babylonian Talmud is, to my mind, akin to *zazen*. And the enthusiastic welcoming of the Shabbat Queen in the synagogue of the

Bratslaver Hasidim in the holy city of Tsfat (Safed in English), where I saw the Sabbath Queen beside my wife, reminds me of the ecstatic *kirtan* chanting of the Hare Krishnas.

Meditation is not just one thing. I tell my students that the word "meditation" is much like the word "exercise." Our concept of exercise joins together such disparate activities as running, playing basketball, gardening, hatha yoga, and lifting weights. All of these activities are different and they develop different parts of the body, but they are alike in that they all enhance the body. In a similar way, specific meditations cultivate different aspects of the mind, but all strengthen the mind. Those who are unfamiliar with meditation wrongly assume that there is only one kind. As the Dalai Lama taught us in Dharamsala, the soulful observance of Shabbat is "your people's visualization exercise."

"Come, My Beloved . . ."

As is often the case, the Dalai Lama with his remarkable insight identified the situation more accurately than anyone else. While many parallels and similarities exist between Jewish and Hindu-Buddhist meditation practices, something about Jewish spirituality is still distinctive. Jewish spirituality is so rooted in this world, in normative Jewish practice. Its most accessible locus is the dining table.

How I wish I could take you by the hand and have you join me at a "Receiving the Sabbath" (*Kabbalat Shabbat*) Friday evening prayer service. In the sixteenth century, led by Rabbi Isaac Luria, known as the Holy Ari, Kabbalists from Spain and North Africa made their way to the holy city of Tsfat in the mountains of northern Israel. The centerpiece of their prayers was the chanted mystical poem *Lekhah Dodi*, "Come, my beloved, let us welcome the Shabbat Bride." Luria taught that when the Romans destroyed the Holy Temple, God's Presence—His female half, known as the *Shekhinah*—went into exile with the Jewish people. Ever since, God above and His bride down here have known the pain of lovers in separation, longing to be reunited, paralleling the longing Jews have always felt for the Land of Israel. Kabbalists understand that their highest task is *tikkun*, to mend, heal, reunify. They evoke the pain of exile in *Lekhah Dodi*: just as a groom longs for his bride, so Jews long for the Shabbat bride, so Hashem longs for the *Shekhinah*.

These days, those who haven't been taught this deeper level of meaning vaguely understand *tikkun* as merely the pursuit of social justice. While that can certainly be an aspect of *tikkun*, it is a despiritualized diminution of a profoundly evocative teaching.

The longing portrayed in *Lekhah Dodi* is the liturgical centerpiece of services for "Receiving the Sabbath" in synagogues around the world. Nowhere is it more powerfully enacted than in the Bratslaver Hasidic synagogue in Tsfat, where a wordless *niggun* dominates the liturgical language. Hundreds of mystics slowly circumambulate the synagogue, clapping hands, some jumping or hopping, all longing for redemption. After prayers, they all return to their homes to sanctify the holy day, bless their children, and have a fine meal attired like nobility. That night, sexual intimacy between husband and wife is a commandment. Analogous to Tantric practices in India, sex is accompanied by meditations on the eternally present third partner in every sanctified and elevated marriage, God Himself.

This, to me, is quintessential Jewish spirituality. It is based on a complex body of knowledge from Biblical, rabbinic, and mystical literature. It is rooted in the earth of human passion transformed into divine service. To engage in its practice, one needs to know a lot—literature, philosophy, languages, and customs. How I wish I could show you what I see, but it involves so much more than just going to Tsfat; it takes years of study to realize the true, deepest meaning of Shabbat.

In India, Ellen and I learned a Shabbat song that the Jews of Cochin sing—"The Day of Shabbat" by an Iraqi liturgist named Mansoor. One line tells it all: "A person untrained in its spirit [i.e., of Shabbat] cannot appreciate it." I wish it were easier, I wish it were more accessible. But perhaps, like all the best things in life, Jewish spirituality takes work, lots of work. But oh, dear reader, how worth it! Just taking the first few steps can open you to Jewish spiritual worlds that cannot even be glimpsed by reading books.

A Script for Mourning

Professional opportunity and discomfort with terrorists aside, the most central factor in our move from Tampa to Miami was the relative quality of Jewish life. Tampa is like most Sunbelt cities: sprawling, disconnected, suburban. While a reasonably large number of Jews live in the area, most are unaffiliated and unconcerned about the things that most matter to me. As one of my colleagues at USF used to put it, in Tampa people live in a climate more than in a community.

We moved to Miami cautiously. Ellen found us a pleasant enough house to rent in a southern suburb, not too far from FIU and very close to a Jewish Community Center (JCC) with a well-deserved reputation for outstanding day care programs. Our precious son was about to turn three, and finding a good Jewish preschool for him was a major concern. Since I had never lived in the suburbs, I was curious about such a typically American experience.

I was pleasantly surprised by the sense of community among our neighbors in our lower-middle-class, racially and culturally diverse enclave. But religiously, we felt alienated. We were searching for our place within the Jewish world. In the suburbs, we attended services at the Young Israel (Orthodox) synagogue, a couple of the Conservative synagogues in our general area, and a Jewish Renewal *havurah* ("fellowship," meaning an alternative-style worship) that met on the University of Miami campus. The *havurah* was led by a deep-thinking, motorcycle-riding mystic, Rabbi Mitch Chefitz. One morning he taught me an elaborate Kabbalistic meditation that accompanies donning *tefillin*. It was a visualization exercise, seeing menorah lights sparking as I wrapped the leather strap around my left forearm and divine names shaped by its coils around my hand. Fairly soon, Ellen and I found that we most enjoyed the Renewal and the Orthodox services.

As the year progressed, we had to decide where to settle. Ellen and I scouted schools in the three areas we were considering, and very quickly Miami Beach emerged as our favorite. Unfortunately, it was also the priciest. In time, we managed to find a rundown place in the heart of the Orthodox community that we could almost afford. Then the question became our fear of living in a "fishbowl," whether our style and level of observance would integrate or alienate us. Despite fears and misgivings, we took the plunge.

During our first year in our new home, my mother passed away, and my period of mourning became a spiritual turning point. Immediately, our neighbors, some of whom we had never even met, delivered meals to us. The rabbi who headed up the *hevrah kaddisha* ("holy brotherhood," the traditional burial society) brought mourner's candles and low seats, as well as a book about the laws of mourning. I learned that one is not permitted to study those laws until the need arises.

When we returned to our Miami Beach home after the funeral in Camden, we found that our meals were delivered by women from the neighborhood without troubling us about logistics. Each morning and afternoon the men came from the synagogue to our home for a *shivah minyan*. I learned that the period between the death of a close relative and the burial is called *aninut*, a time of ritually bound intense grief and bewilderment when even the most basic laws, such as the requirement to offer morning prayers, are suspended. You are left to confront the reality of death starkly. *Shivah* (literally, seven) is observed for seven days after the funeral. For this week, you wear the garment torn by the rabbi at the time of burial, you sit on a low chair, and you recite the memorial prayer with a quorum (*minyan*) in your home, which you do not leave. When that is over, you observe eleven months of thrice-daily memorial prayers in the synagogue.

The custom is to pay a *shivah* call on someone who is in mourning. Like almost everyone, I always felt so awkward at the news of the death of a friend's relative. I wanted to do something, but didn't know what; I wanted to say something, but I had no words. A traditional way of life, especially in Orthodoxy, provides the script. The mourner sits on a low chair, and visitors come and sit by her or his side, saying nothing, not even a greeting. If the mourner wishes to speak, the visitor responds, perhaps asking a question about the departed, the assumption being that it is cathartic to express your grief by discussing your memories of the lost loved one. The visitor stays only briefly, and upon departure intones the traditional words of comfort that have been recited ever since mourners used to visit the Holy Temple after getting up from their *shivah*: "May Hashem comfort you among the mourners of Zion and Jerusalem." No one was either awkward or self-conscious, because everyone knew exactly what was expected. Tradition provided a script to enable everyone, mourner and comforter, to navigate one of life's most distressing episodes with dignity and grace.

Day after day, women brought meals, on the assumption that preparing food, while essential, was beyond a family's capacity during this intense time. Our freezer was stuffed with enough food for a month. Each morning Ellen set up an urn of coffee, some pastry, herring, and cheese for the men who came for the prayers. After prayers I would sit on the low seat and the men would sit by my side, keeping me company in silence if I wished, or responding sympathetically to my memories of my mother. One by one, each would ceremoniously stand before me as a *menahem* (comforter) offering the ancient formula, then leave. One or two would linger. Some of the regulars at my *shivah minyan* have since become close friends.

When it was time to get up from the *shivah*, I knew that I had truly found a home in Miami Beach. By the time I had finished saying *Kaddish* (the memorial prayer, recited for eleven months and on the death anniversary, or *yortsayt*, forever thereafter), I was emotionally ready to move on. My admiration for the profundity of Jewish tradition knew no bounds because I realized fully how it had transported me through my crisis by providing a script for my suffering. As a scholar once wrote, religion's purpose is not so much to remove suffering from human experience, because it is fundamentally ineradicable, but to make suffering sufferable.

A Script for Living

To live out your emotions within a community is to live a life scripted by a divine author. I realize how high-falutin' that sounds, but I can think of no better metaphor for the deep appeal Orthodoxy holds for me. When people lift a glass of single malt Scotch at a wedding or bar-mitzvah, the most frequent toast is "Only *simhahs!*" (joyous events). We Jews know as well as anyone that life is not only *simhah*, but this formula expresses affirmation in the face of absurdity. Even one of our best-known wedding rituals, the breaking of a glass, reminds us that the dark side is never far away, that we remain in mourning for the Holy Temple even as we celebrate life.

We Jews count our days in relation to the Sabbath. That is, Sunday is not Sunday, but the "first day" (*yom rishon*) after Shabbat. We live from Shabbat to Shabbat. We mark time by our festivals and fasts. By mooring our calendar in the sacred, we make all of time potentially sanctified.

Booths and Blessings

When we first moved to suburban Miami, autumn and Sukkot, the festival of booths, came in due course after the New Year and Yom Kippur. A friend of ours called to ask whether we had yet built our *sukkah*, a gaily decorated little booth outdoors in which Jews eat and celebrate for the week of the holiday. We had never built one before, and our friend, always zealous to perform a *mitzvah*, a divine command, showed up with a *sukkah* in the back of his truck, which we proceeded to erect and decorate. The year before she died, my mother visited during this most joyous of Jewish celebrations. She reminded me that her father, my pious grandfather in Camden, built a tiny *sukkah* annually in the alley beside his row house. Ever since that year, helped by my friend's practical encouragement, we have erected our own *sukkah*.

In Jewish schools, children make decorations for the *sukkah*. We string New Year's cards together and hang them, and we shop for religiously themed waterproof posters and pictures. Autumn is the rainy season in Florida, and we only wish there were a way to waterproof the entire *sukkah*! One year we spent Sukkot in Israel, where the holiday falls during the dry season, and Rafi and I were able for the first time to sleep as well as eat and celebrate in the booth. After synagogue prayers during the first two and last two days of Sukkot, people in our community go "*sukkah* hopping" after lunch, visiting friends and neighbors for a drink or a bite of cake, but mostly for holy camaraderie.

In America, Jews of relatively marginal observance annually confront a "December dilemma," which is how they describe their children's envy of the beauty, bustle, and bounty of Christmas, especially when compared with the attenuated observance of Hanukkah. It's understandable: a *latke* (potato pancake) doesn't hold a proverbial candle to a ham and turkey feast, and even eight nights of gifts do not measure up to the majesty of Christmas music, or even the storied presence of Santa Claus in the malls. But once you have experienced the joys of a *sukkah*, how can you be jealous of a Christmas tree? Dwelling in a *sukkah* is like living *inside* a Christmas tree, fairy lights and all!

Ever since my first fitful visit to Jerusalem during Sukkot 1976, I have felt a need to somehow repair the embarrassment in my heart. In modern times, Israel experiences a partial reenactment of the great pilgrimage festival that Sukkot once was, when every Jew in Eretz Israel, theoretically at least, went to the Holy Temple to offer sacrifices and celebrate the Presence of God. I had seen photographs of the Kotel, the sole remaining wall of the ancient Temple, on the first of the intermediate days of Sukkot. On this day, tens of thousands of Jews go to the Kotel. The high point of the service is when thousands of hereditary priests (*kohanim*) give the priestly benediction to the people. As a *kohen*, it became one of my heart's deepest wishes to participate in this, one of the most ancient rituals in this most ancient religion.

In 2003 I had that opportunity, and my family and I rode a crowded public bus to the Old City and made our way to the already-jammed Kotel Plaza. Ellen went to the women's section, while Rafi and I had to push and shove our way to the front of the men's area, where the *kohanim* would perform the rite of blessing the crowd. Newspapers the next day reported that fifty thousand people crowded themselves into the plaza, and I assume about a tenth of them were hereditary priests.

After lengthy prayers, our time came. We placed our prayer shawls over our heads, made the sacred gesture with our *tallit*-enfolded hands, and readied ourselves. Even before anything was said or done, I could feel wave after wave of intense energy cascading down from the Temple Mount, electrifying my body. The prayer leader intoned the threefold blessing over a loudspeaker, to be repeated by five thousand priests: "May Hashem bless you and safeguard you," and forty-five thousand voices roared "Amen." The response was even more powerful than the divine energy that I could feel flowing through me. The next verse followed: "May Hashem illuminate His countenance for you and be gracious to you," and the cascade seemed to amplify tenfold. It felt to me as though the blessing were passing through me with such force that my personality dissolved, that the very cells of my flesh were awash with the power of the Divine Presence. The thunderous "Amen" was likewise amplified. The third verse, "May Hashem turn his countenance to you and establish peace for you," followed, and as the especially blessed final word, "Shalom," came through my throat and my heart and my being, I felt my fragmented self merge with not only the fifty thousand who were present, not only the fifteen million Jews in the world, but also with everything that God has ever created—past, present, and future! The response of "Amen" likewise enveloped all the world, and I believe that for the first time in my life, I felt, I became, that Peace which has been God's promise ever since this blessing was first revealed to Aaron, the brother of Moses and the first *kohen*.

And all of this took place while Rafi and I were being jostled, pushed, and shoved by countless rude yeshiva students who felt entitled to the very spot where we were standing! It is truly amazing how spirituality can make one accept good-naturedly the petty annoyances that make up far too much of our mundane lives. It also teaches me that Jewish spirituality is not a removal from, nor a negation of, mundane reality, but is achieved by seeing the divine within the mundane. What could be more divine than channeling this ancient benediction, and what could be more mundane than being rudely jostled? And where else could they be so fully harmonized than here in Jerusalem, and when other than during Sukkot, this season of our joy (*zeman simhatenu*)?

Mourning Without Melancholia

The most somber day of the Jewish calendar is Tishah be-Av, a fast to memorialize the multiple tragedies in Jewish history that occurred on this date: the destruction of both the First and Second Temples, the expulsion from Spain, and, in modern times, the Shoah (the Hebrew term for the Holocaust). Synagogues are darkened, worshippers sit on low benches like mourners. The readings consist of the Book of Lamentations, which describes the woeful condition of our beloved Jerusalem after the Babylonians burned it. Listening to the text is excruciating, for it even describes tender mothers, frenzied by starvation, cannibalizing their own dear children. Other elegies (*kinnot*) describe in gruesome detail the martyrdom of holy Rabbi Akiva, whose skin was flayed with metal combs before he was wrapped in a Torah scroll and set ablaze, following which his cruel tormentors doused him with just enough water to prolong his suffering. Tishah be-Av is a descent into the abyss, from nightfall to nightfall.

Yet, as the day moves into afternoon, the liturgy turns to consolation and the hope for redemption. We read the message of the prophets, that even in the midst of the most horrible afflictions imaginable, God may be hidden, but He is not absent, and He will return to us as He will return us to Jerusalem. This drama of torture and redemption pervades not only the day of Tishah be-Av, but the whole cycle of prophetic readings. The weeks of mourning before Tishah be-Av are punctuated with readings of warnings. After Tishah be-Av comes the Sabbath of Comfort, *Shabbat Nahamu*, and seven weeks of hopeful readings leading up to the New Year and all its promises. Such a calendar reflects our own spiritual experiences as our souls spiral ever upward on their journeys toward union with God; over thousands of years, liturgy and psyche have been synchronized.

In some senses, Tishah be-Av is my "favorite" holy day. I don't think I am an especially morbid person, but there is something profound about facing the abyss directly, with no veneer, and then emerging. Just as a fast is purifying, so, too, this liturgy is cathartic. By the time the prayers finish and the fast ends late in the evening, one makes *Kiddush* and heartily partakes of nourishment for the body to parallel the nourishment for the soul found in the liturgy.

I found it especially incongruous one year to mark Tishah be-Av in Jerusalem. Of course, I went to the Old City, and heard Lamentations read in the Churva Synagogue, once the most elegant in all of Jerusalem, a building that was demolished and desecrated during the Jordanian occupation. The synagogue has not been reconstructed, so that its remnants stand as a reminder of our history. It seemed to me that hearing about the Roman sack of Jerusalem in a destroyed synagogue would be particularly apt, but it wasn't. The roofless structure enabled me to see a thriving Jewish city all around me. Even more than in America, I felt distant from the events of two millennia past that were being lamented. As soon as the reading was over, I strolled to the nearby Kotel. I searched within for despair, for mourning over the destroyed Temple. But as I gazed at its one remaining retaining wall, with thousands of Jews milling about, despite myself, I felt a sense of joy and uplift. That year, I did not find consolation in the liturgy, but in my very presence in Jerusalem.

Mourning and joy, work and rest, death and life. Living an observant life teaches me that you cannot attain spirituality by negating the former for the latter, but in moving from one to another with the ease that comes from having a script.

The Dalai Lama in Miami

We were just unpacking boxes at our new home in Miami Beach on a hot Sunday afternoon in August 1995, when the phone rang. It was the Dalai Lama! He was at the Miami Airport Hotel between flights en route to South America. Would I like to stop by for a visit? Ellen, Rafael, and I washed, dressed, and zoomed over. As is always the case with the Dalai Lama, it was a delightful visit. I am not entirely sure what prompted me, but with no authority whatsoever, I invited His Holiness to visit my new university—I had taught there for just a year—to receive an honorary doctorate. He agreed to come.

So I was nervous when I called Florida International University's president on Monday morning. "Sir, you will never guess what I did. I invited the Dalai Lama to come to FIU for an honorary degree." Mitch Maidique, truly a visionary leader in what is normally a domain of groupthink, responded with enthusiasm, but reminded me that I had entirely bypassed procedures for honorary degrees. I knew that. We backtracked through the proper channels, and the Dalai Lama's historic first official visit to Florida took place in 1999.

The scale of the event—security was intense, complex, and expensive; more than fifty television crews were credentialed; ticket distribution was chaotic—was overwhelming, but it went off flawlessly. It truly amazed me how each of the five thousand people who attended felt such a strong connection to one of the greatest spiritual teachers in the world.

Just before the program, His Holiness and I were sitting in the "green room" when he smiled, arched an eyebrow, and asked, "So, what should I talk about?" I replied that since my religious studies department was backing the event, perhaps he could talk about religion and public life, and religion in the context of a public university.

In his remarks, he said that each person has two complementary sides, a social self and an individual self. As his social self, he taught, when he is with people of other faiths, he can readily appreciate how religions make people better, how they inculcate generosity and compassion. In this respect, we can see that all religions have similar results. What he said was precisely what the third-century B.C.E. Buddhist emperor of India, the great Ashoka Maurya, had taught. Ashoka's multireligious polity could serve as a model for the world even today. On the other hand, the Dalai Lama continued, for himself, as an individual who is Buddhist, he believes that Buddhism is the best possible religion. People need such certainty to arise at 4:00 a.m. to meditate, as he does. People need that kind of strengthening for the hard work that all genuine spirituality requires. Typical of him, his words went right into my heart.

He said that modern universities do an excellent job of training the good brain, but perhaps not such a good job of training the warm heart. Intellect devoid of heart can be arrogant and even destructive, because a warm heart devoid of keen intellect can be merely sentimental. So a combination of some kind would be best, some way of training the good brain and the warm heart.

I pondered his message for years afterward, and in response to it, I recently started FIU's Center for the Study of Spirituality, which promises to be a unique academic undertaking.[2] Its vision, inspired by the Dalai Lama and culled from conversations with people of all faiths as well as some of no particular faith, is to begin with the traditions of spirituality in the world's religions, but to extend that range to include contemporary "secular" applications of spirituality in such disparate realms as medicine and the health sciences, clinical psychology, education, the fine and performing arts, architecture, environmental studies, tourism, business, international relations, creative writing, and on and on. We don't know yet whether our new center will succeed, although we have already been approved to offer the nation's first minor in the study of spirituality, but, as they say, the path is itself the goal, so the effort is its own reward.

Leaving Nothing Behind

It may be obvious, but I feel I need to emphasize that my journey, from a lukewarm, traditional Jewish home, to Sufis and ashrams and meditation centers in Asia, and then to Orthodox Judaism, doesn't mean that I reject anything at all. To the chagrin of many of my Orthodox friends, I maintain strong connections in the Hindu and Buddhist worlds, as must be obvious to anyone who has read this far.

For example, not long ago I reached one of those spiritual barriers in my morning prayers when I felt I was merely reciting lifeless words. I knew there was no real alternative but to keep praying. I took my family to a Hindu ashram in nearby Sebastian, Florida. The guru is Brooklyn-born (as is obvious the moment she speaks), Ma Jayasati Bhagavati, an eccentric, eclectic, enthusiastic, and controversial teacher. I told Ma about my block, and she suggested that I *daven* (yes, Ma was born Jewish, an identity she affirms) not only on the out-breath and the in-breath, but also on the no-breath. I had some experience of the no-breath from practicing *kundalini* yoga, so the next Monday morning I *davened* as she had suggested, and it worked. On the in-breath the Divine enters us, and on the out-breath we merge with the Divine. And on the

---

[2] See the center's website, http://spirituality.fiu.edu.

no-breath, as Ma suggested, we find the silence that the Hindus call the identity of the universal self and the individual self, or Brahman and Atman, and that the Tibetans call the Clear Light, and that we Jews understand as the Fathomless *Ein-Sof,* the before-Creation and the after-Redemption condition, perfect, complete, the Light that as I child I glimpsed emanating from the Holy Ark. From time to time, I still return to this technique to enliven my prayers.

One fine Sunday morning, we responded to an invitation from some Sikh friends to visit their *gurudwara* (temple) in Broward County. We enjoyed the melodious chanting from their holy book, and afterward we joined our friends for a tasty vegetarian meal. Many people came to greet us and chat, but I was very surprised when one of the Sikh teenagers greeted me in Hebrew. "Where did you learn our language?" I asked, and he told me he had spent a semester at the Alexander Muss High School in Hod Ha-Sharon, Israel. "How did you happen to go there?" He replied that most of his friends in high school were Jewish, so he decided to join them in their Israeli immersion program!

Return of the Dalai Lama

The ten days of repentance between Rosh Hashanah and Yom Kippur are a time for Jews to go inward, to realign themselves with God, and to make amends for any problems with their family and neighbors. This process of "returning" to God is known as *teshuvah,* repentance.

It might seem inappropriate that I spent several of these ten days during 2004 with the Dalai Lama, but no one has ever taught me more about "returning"—returning to the religion of my birth, Judaism, a religion which I have come to understand as perfectly attuned to my soul.

We all know that what we *do* is more important than what we *say.* But recently, a new lesson was impressed on me: that what we *are* may be even more important than what we *do.*

Recently, I participated in a Tibetan-Jewish dialogue at The Temple, Atlanta's leading Reform synagogue, which boasts the distinction of having been firebombed during the civil rights movement, as portrayed in *Driving Miss Daisy.* I was to share the podium with my good friend of many years, the Venerable Dr. Geshe Lobsang Tendzin Negi. Geshe-la, as he is respectfully known, has attained the pinnacle of Tibetan monastic education, the esteemed *geshe lharampa* degree, as well as a Ph.D. in psychology from Emory University. To say that he has an insightful mind is an understatement. Moreover, he is a witty and sincere gentleman who has been a guest in my home as well as in my synagogue.

In our public dialogue, Geshe-la recounted our experiences with one another's people and religion. We talked about similarities between Judaism and Tibetan Buddhism, the esoteric threads of Kabbalah and Tantra in particular. We covered the difficult topic of Jews who forsake the way of their ancestors to follow Tibetan teachings, and we discussed the Tibetan people's heroic struggle to preserve their culture in exile, having been forced to abandon their majestic homeland due to ruthless Chinese occupation since the 1950s.

We opened the crowded floor to engage the audience. Seated on posh wing chairs, we responded to questions, some naive, some profound. We talked about meditation and shared the pain of exile. Learning the Dalai Lama's never-before-asked, poignant question—"What is the Jewish secret for preserving a religion and a culture while in exile?"—the audience focused even more on our words. How did we do it? What did you tell the Dalai Lama? Why hasn't anyone ever asked us before?

Hearing about the United Nations' heartless silence and lack of response to the Tibetan plight, one man in the audience could stand it no longer. He rose to his feet, red-eyed, pained. He asked Geshe-la, "What can we Jews do to help you Tibetans? Should we try to lobby the UN to take up your cause? Ought we work through the U.S. Congress?" He reminded Geshe-la about American Jewry's political strength, suggesting that we commence a lobbying effort on behalf of the Tibetans. "Just tell us what we can do to help," he implored.

Geshe-la's response was immediate. "Nothing," he said. "You don't have to do anything. Just be who you are, just be Jews." I smiled a deep smile as the interlocutor turned left and right in bafflement. The *geshe* was gracious enough to elaborate. "You cannot imagine how much encouragement we take from you, just for being who you are. The fact that you are still here, the fact that you still worship in your way—this means more to us than anything you could possibly do. You are a great source of strength to us, and we are grateful to you."

Just like that, Geshe-la revealed our own wisdom to us.

Our sages teach that there are two kinds of *mitzvot* (commandments). One kind establishes the vertical connection between humans and God, and the other establishes the horizontal connections among people. The former are ritual *mitzvot* like prayer, laying *tefillin*, keeping kosher, observing Shabbat and holy days, and taking other steps that link us to the transcendent. The latter are ethical *mitzvot*: the thou-shalts and thou-shalt-nots, the laws of marriage, inheritance, contracts, and those laws that make for a peaceful and just society. Today, our fractious religion has largely relegated the ritual *mitzvot* to the Orthodox, while the Reform commandeer the ethical *mitzvot*. Many Jews seem to tie the sacred task of "mending the world," or *tikkun ha-olam*, only to the ethical *mitzvot*, relegating the ritual *mitzvot* to the socially meaningless category of "spirituality."

But a genuine spirituality, such as Geshe-la's, knows no such bifurcation of religion. In this case, we help to mend the world precisely by fulfilling our ritual obligations. The *mitzvot* and responsibility of mending are much deeper than social policy. Or, to put it another way, we can never fulfill our ceaseless task of mending if we only look outside, at externals. Authentic spirituality transforms not merely the individual but, in truth, has the power to transform the very world. And *that* is *tikkun ha-olam*, nothing less.

I'm beating around the bush. The sixth-century B.C.E. Chinese sage Lao Tzu said it with an exquisite economy of verbiage: "The way to do is to be."

Afterword

∼

Why I'm Here

In Orthodox Judaism, I find a worldview that places piety above profession, and this especially appeals to me at a very deep level as a high-achieving, professionally oriented modern person. A professor's life is keenly competitive and often backbiting, so I find this more spiritual orientation to be refreshing. In fact, the academic world has been one of my life's disappointments. I am still passionate about students, teaching, research, and writing, and wish that was all there is to being a professor. But life in the university follows Henry Kissinger's wry aphorism: "University politics are so nasty precisely because the stakes are so low." I have always lived as far away as possible—geographically, socially, and psychologically—from the campus,

I discovered Jewish spirituality by way of Hinduism and Buddhism, and would go so far as to say that my experiences with these "alien" paths gave me the eyes to see my own religion anew. Meditation enabled me to see what was always in front of my face. When seen with such eyes, with Dharma eyes, the vast system of rituals of Orthodox Judaism points me directly toward the sanctity of the everyday, the sacredness of the mundane. The table in my dining room is now sacred: it *is* the altar of the Temple. Again and again, the swamis and lamas I so deeply admired pointed me in this unexpected direction: back home.

Trungpa Rinpoche gave me a piece of calligraphy that hangs above my desk in my home office. The name he bestowed on me when I took the vows of the *bodhisattva* is written in a powerful Tibetan script. It says Lodro Lhaö, "divine light of intellect." I feel that those powerful vows, based on Shantideva's fervent poetry, still sustain me, vows that are perfectly reflected in the teaching of the Lubavitcher Rebbe:

> No man can claim to have reached the ultimate truth as long as there
> is another who has not.
> No one is redeemed until we are all redeemed.
> Ultimate truth is an unlimited light
> —and if it is unlimited, how could it shine in one person's realm and
> not in another's?

I also felt strongly drawn by the way Orthodox men relate to their children. I had never even imagined such closeness, such open affection, such effective role-modeling. I have always been a hands-on father, but until now I had always felt somewhat isolated. I was not a stay-at-home dad, but neither was I the stereotypical professional for whom children ranked somewhere below professional achievement, wealth, and Sunday football games. That women and men pray separately, which while not a simple issue, reflects what I understand feminism to teach about the importance of establishing a woman-centered community. Ellen tells me that the Orthodox way of gender arrangements, when practiced in a marriage of real mutual respect and affection, exalts both women and men. Of course, in cases where the marriage is troubled, these same arrangements can be used to oppress women cruelly, but perhaps our community's challenge is to work on the marriage first and the arrangements second.

I feel that I now live in a world whose values better reflect my own, or perhaps more accurately, whose values I more wish to emulate. The surprise is that these are the same values that mattered to me most during my childhood, my adolescent rebellion, and my adult spiritual quest. Far from negating my journey, my new life is a continuation of what I learned in Camden and in Benares, in Dharamsala and in Jerusalem: piety and family, spirituality and meaningful action in the world.

Glossary

~

arti (Sanskrit). A form of Hindu worship in which a lighted lamp (*deepak* or *diva*) is waved before an image of a deity. Also known as *arartika*, which means the waving of lights before the image.

ahdut (Hebrew). Unity.

Advaita Vedanta (Sanskrit). A Hindu non-dualistic system of thought and mysticism, chiefly expounded by the eighth-century mystical philosopher Shankaracharya. *Advaita* means non-dual, and *Vedanta* literally means the concluding portion of the Vedas.

am ha-aretz (Hebrew). "Person of the earth." A common person, an ignoramus.

amrit (Sanskrit). "Undying," the nectar of immortality, ambrosia. *Dudtsi* in Tibetan.

anima (Latin). Soul. In Jungian psychology, it is the presentation of the unconscious in female form.

aninut (Hebrew). The period of most intense grief from the moment of a close relative's death until burial. The mourner is called an *onen.*

arahant, arhat (Pali, Sanskrit). A "worthy one," a fully enlightened disciple of the Buddha.

Aramaic. The language of the Talmud, the spoken language of Israel in the centuries before and after the beginning of the first millennium, a lingua franca from the Mediterranean to the Indus River.

Arbhith (Hebrew). Sephardic designation for evening prayers.

Aron ha-Kodesh (Hebrew). Holy Ark where Torah scrolls are stored in synagogues.

Ashkenazi (from Hebrew *Ashkenaz*, Germany). Jews of East European origin.

ashram (Sanskrit). "Place of striving," a hermitage or the residence of a guru and his or her disciples.

Atman (Sanskrit). The innermost soul.

avodah (Hebrew). Can mean either "work" or "worship." Cf. Sanskrit *karma*.

avodah zarah (Hebrew). "Foreign worship," approximated in English as idolatry.

Ayyah (Sinhala). "Sister," a respectful form of address for a Buddhist nun.

baal-tefillah (Hebrew). Leader of the prayers.

baal-teshuvah (Hebrew' pl. **baalei-teshuvah**). A "master of the return," a Jew who becomes observant. In the jargon, a "BT."

beit-din (Hebrew; pl. *batei-din*). "House of judgment," a rabbinic court.

Baha'i. A monotheistic religion of Persian origin that grew out of Shi'a Islam in the nineteenth century. The world headquarters of Baha'i is in Haifa, Israel.

bar-mitzvah (Hebrew). "Son of the commandments," a young man at the age of thirteen attains this status of moral responsibility. Often the term for a coming-of-age ritual for a Jewish boy; a parallel status, *bat-mitzvah*, is given to young women at the age of twelve (Orthodox) or thirteen (non-Orthodox).

Bayit ha-Rishon (Hebrew). "The First House," the Temple of Solomon; *the Bayit ha-Sheni*, or " Second House," was the Second Temple.

be-di-avad (Aramaic). "after the fact," *ex post facto*.

Bene Israel. The largest Jewish community in India. Of uknown origin, the Bene Israel were once known as "Saturday oil-pressers" (*Shanwar Teli*) who refrained from work on the Sabbath. They practiced circumcision on a baby's eighth day, and recited the first line of the *Shema* whenever prayer was appropriate. Over the past two and a half centuries, they underwent a remarkable transformation into modern, urban Jews.

bhajan (Sanskrit). A popular spiritual song.

bimah (Hebrew). Pulpit.

bikkurim (Hebrew). The annual harvest's "first fruits," which were offered at the Temple in Jerusalem.

Birkat ha-Mazon (Hebrew). "Blessing of the meal," recited after eating.

bodhisattva (Sanskrit). "Enlightenment-hero," the ideal of human perfection in northern or Mahayana Buddhism.

berakhah (Hebrew). A blessing or benediction.

Brahman (Sanskrit). The transcendent essence of the universe, traditionally described with the words *Sat-Chit-Ananda*, "Truth, Consciousness, and Bliss."

Brahmin (Sanskrit). A hereditary priest. The highest caste among Hindus, Brahmins are invested with the sacred thread in a ceremony known *upanayana samskara*, when the guru initiates the disciple with the famous Gayatri mantra.

be-tzelem E-lokim (Hebrew). "In the image of God." In the Genesis creation narrative, it is said that Adam and Eve were created *be-tzelem E-lokim* (Genesis 1:27).

Buddha, Buddhism. Buddhism is a major world religion based on the compassionate and selfless teachings of Siddhartha Gautama, who became known as "the Enlightened One" or the Buddha. Begun in India during the sixth century BCE, Buddhism spread throughout Asia but all but vanished in its homeland.

Chazzan (Hebrew). A cantor; *chazzanut* is the term for the cantorial arts.

chené (Tibetan). Dyed grains of rice that function as a protective talisman.

Chevrah Kaddisha (Hebrew, Aramaic). "Holy brotherhood," the traditional, voluntary burial society that performs the rites to prepare the corpse for burial.

Chögyal (Tibetan; *Dharmaraja* in Sanskrit). An ideal Buddhist king who rules in accordance with Dharma (righteousness).

chorten (Tibetan; *stupa* in Sanskrit). A bell-shaped reliquary, ubiquitous in the Buddhist world, containing remains of the Buddha or a Buddhist saint.

chutzpah (Hebrew). Audaciousness, bravery. (Adj. *chutspedik*, Yiddish).

daf yomi (Hebrew). "A page a day." A system for reading the entire Talmud, one page a day for seven and a half years.

dakini (Sanskrit). "She who goes in the sky," a female deity who inspires Buddhist adepts. In Tibetan, *khendroma*.

dal (Hindi). Lentil stew.

darbar (Hindustani). A public court of a secular or religious leader.

davenen (Yiddish). To pray.

deity-yoga. A Tantric Buddhist meditation wherein the meditator visualizes an aspect of enlightenment and appropriates the symbolized wisdom.

derekh eretz (Hebrew). "The way of the world." Courtesy, conventional morality, social relationships, the workaday world.

dharamshala (Sanskrit). A rest house for pilgrims. Also the name of a town in the Himalayan foothills, seat of the Tibetan government-in-exile.

Dharma (Sanskrit). Highly multivalent word, which depending on context could mean Truth, a teaching, social duty, social order, an irreducible factor in human experience. Hindus call their religion Sanantana Dharma (eternal Dharma), and Buddhists often call theirs simply Buddha-Dharma.

Dharma center. A meditation-oriented Buddhist center, usually in the west.

Dhikr (Arabic and Aramaic [*dekhir*]). See *mantra*.

dudtsi (Tibetan). Nectar of immortality, ambrosia. In Sanskrit, *amrit.*

Eelam (Tamil). The name for a proposed Tamil state in northern and eastern Sri Lanka.

Ein-Sof (Hebrew). "The Fathomless," the transcendent God in Lurianic Kabbalah.

eshet hayil (Hebrew). A "virtuous woman"; from a song attributed to King Solomon (Proverbs 31:10–31) that the husband (and sometimes others) chants to the wife before the Friday evening meal.

Habad (Hebrew). An acronym for the three levels of wisdom: *hokhmah, binah,* and *da'at.* The name of a Hasidic sect also known as Lubavitch.

Hakham (Hebrew, pl. **hakhamim**). A wise man, Sephardic term for a rabbi.

Galut ha-Shekhinah (Hebrew). The "exile of God's presence," a teaching that a part of God's immanence went into exile (*galut*) along with the Jewish people, often symbolized as female.

Gam zu le-tovah (Hebrew). "This, too, is for the good" (*Ta'anit* 21a; *Sanhedrin* 108b–109a).

Ganga (Sanskrit). "River," or more properly Mata Ganga, "the Mother River," Hinduism's most sacred river. Lord Shiva is said to carry Ganga in the tuft of his matted hair The British called this sacred river the Ganges.

ghat (Hindustani). A place of descent to a river, a landing place for a ferry, rather like a contemporary river-walk.

gilgul nefesh (Hebrew). Transmigration or reincarnation.

guru (Sanskrit). A teacher, often a spiritual teacher.

gurudwara (Punjabi). A Sikh house of worship. *Gurudwara* literally means a doorway to the great guru, where Sikhism's sacred text, the *Guru Granth Sahib*, is recited.

"Gut Shabbos" (Yiddish). "A good Sabbath," a greeting on the Sabbath.

Hadran (Hebrew). "Encore! Let us repeat," a verbal proclamation made upon completing a Talmudic tractate to indicate the hope of returning and relearning the material just completed.

Halakhah (Hebrew). "The way," the system of Judaic law (adj. *halakhic*).

Hashem (Hebrew). Literally "The Name," the term by which Orthodox Jews refer to God.

Hasidism. "Pietists," the name of a movement for religious and spiritual revival among East European Jewry from the eighteen century. Often contrasted with the northern European rationalists who dominated rabbinical seminaries.

havurah (Hebrew). In contemporary American Judaism, informal prayer and study groups that often substitute for synagogues.

heshbon ha-nefesh (Hebrew). "Accounting the soul," a spiritual-meditative practice for improving one's character traits (*middot*).

Heymish (Yiddish). "Homey," familiar, comfortable.

Hinayana (Sanskrit). "Inferior vehicle," a pejorative term applied in Mahayana polemics against other Buddhists.

Hindu, Hinduism. "Hinduism" is the name applied to the diverse religious sects and customs of the subcontinent. The earliest use of the term "Hindu" (*Hindu'a*) is found in the Babylonian Talmud to refer to a person or product from geographic region that roughly corresponds to the India of the British era.

hiyuv (Hebrew). Obligation in religious or ethical matters.

hol ha-moed (Hebrew). The intermediate days of the festivals of Sukkot and Pesach—half ordinary (*hol*), half holy (*moed*).

huppah (Hebrew). Canopy used in a wedding ceremony.

I Ching (Chinese). One of the five classical text of Confucianism, used for divination.

Jain. A Jain is a follower of the religion known as Jainism in English, based on the formulation of the sixth century BCE teacher, Mahavira. An ascetic path for lay and monastics alike, the concept of "non-harm" or *ahimsa* originated in this tradition and was adapted by many religions of India, especially the modern form of Hinduism taught by Mahatma Gandhi.

jhana, dhyana (Pali, Sanskrit). A form of meditation emphasizing withdrawal of consciousness from the senses, often called "trance meditation."

Kabbalah (Hebrew). "That which is received." Jewish mysticism.

Kabbalat Shabbat (Hebrew). "Receiving the Sabbath," the prayer service at the commencement of the Sabbath on Friday evenings.

Kaddish (Aramaic, Hebrew). "Sanctification." A series of prayers in Aramaic, the best-known of which is the mourner's *Kaddish*.

Kaddish de-Rabbanan (Aramaic). "Sanctification for scholars." A form of the *Kaddish* recited after a session of learning sacred texts.

kadosh (Aramaic, Hebrew). "Holy," a Biblical exclamation.

Kagyüdpa (Tibetan). "Those who continue the Word." One of the four main Tibetan Buddhist sects.

Kalachakra Tantra (Sanskrit). The "cycle of time" Tantra. A text and a system of esoteric Buddhist meditation.

karma (Sanskrit). Work or ritual activity. The root of the word is *kri*, which means "to do"; it is therefore an act of performance. From the religious point of view, *karma* means any sacrifice or oblation done for a deceased person. Cf. Hebrew *avodah*.

Kashi (Sanskrit). "Light," a classical name for the holiest Hindu city, Benares (now known as Varanasi). It is related to the word Prakash, which stands for Lord Shiva, and Kashi is also the City of Lord Shiva, Kashi Vishwanath, "the Light that is Lord of the Universe."

Kasina (Pali). An meditational object used to enhance concentration.

katha (Tibetan). A ceremonial long white scarf presented to an exalted person during an introduction.

kavvanah (Hebrew). "Intention," the inner state of mind that accompanies a religious obligation (*mitzvah*).

Kiddush Hashem (Hebrew). "Sanctification of the Name." Behaviors that bring credit to one's religion, including martyrdom, or dying with God in one's mind and on one's lips.

kippah (Hebrew; pl. *kippot*). A skullcap, called in Yiddish a *yarmulke* (variously spelled). A *kippah serugah* is a knitted *kippah* worn by men who consider themselves Modern Orthodox, as distinct from velvet *kippot*, worn by the strictly-Orthodox *haredim*.

kirtan (Hindi). A Hindu devotional song based on the names of the Divine, usually accompanied with a *mridanga*, *tabla* and *sitar*, and other musical instruments.

koan (Japanese). A riddle taken as a focus for meditation in Zen practice.

kohen, kohanim (Hebrew). A hereditary priest, a patrilineal descendant of Aaron, brother of Moses.

kohen gadol (Hebrew). The high priest.

Kol Nidrei (Aramaic). "All vows." The chant that begins the prayers on Yom Kippur, the Day of Atonement, the holiest day of the Jewish year.

kosher (Hebrew). "Fitting" or "appropriate." Designates foods that may be eaten according to Halakhah.

Kotel (Hebrew). "Wall," especially the *Kotel ha-Ma'aravi*, the Western Wall, the only remaining structure from the ancient Temple. The holiest site in Judaism, it is said to be the foundation from which the Temple will be rebuilt.

kovil (Tamil). A Hindu temple.

kundalini (Sanskrit). The psycho-physical energy said to travel the spinal column, according to esoteric Hinduism. She is the serpentine coil of three and half whirls, going from the base of the spine, the *muladhara*, to the crown of the head, or *sahsrara*, to awaken the dormant energy, through the spinal cord, the *sushumna*. Kundalini is an esoteric Tantric practice.

kurta-pyjama (Hindustani). The loose-fitting, long cotton shirt and trousers widely worn by men in northern India.

lama (Tibetan). "Superior one"; in Sanskrit, *guru*.

latihan (Indonesian). A system of mediation in Subud, an esoteric Indonesian offshoot of Islam.

Lekhah Dodi (Hebrew). "Come, my beloved." A liturgical song sung at the beginning of the Sabbath wherein the Sabbath is welcomed in the form of a mystical Queen.

Le-kha-tehillah (Hebrew). "At the outset"; *ab initio*.

Longchen Nyingthig (Tibetan). A system of meditation in Tibetan Buddhism founded by Longchenpa, a prolific author and mystic of the fourteenth century.

Lurianic Kabbalah. The esoteric system taught by Rabbi Isaac Luria (1534–1572), popularly known as the Ari or the Arizal. Luria's teachings, based on the

Zohar, the foundational text of Jewish mysticism, were compiled in a work known as the *Etz Hayyim*. Luria lived most of his life in Tsfat (Safed), the center for Kabbalah, and the influence of his mystical theology is deep and widespread.

mahasiddha (Sanskrit). "Great accomplished one," the wonder-working esoteric images of human perfection in Tantric Buddhism.

Mahayana Buddhism. The dominant form of Buddhist in northern and eastern Asia, emphasizing the modeling and salvific power of the enlightenment-hero known as the *bodhisattva*.

Mahavamsa (Pali). "The Great Chronicle," composed in fifth-century Sri Lanka, detailing the idealized early history of Buddhism there.

mantra (Sanskrit). "Mind-protector," sacred words of mystical and magical power that confer benefits when recited. Cf. *dhikr* in Hebrew and Arabic.

Masjid, masajid (Arabic). A Muslim house of worship, commonly called *mosque* in English.

matzah (Hebrew). Unleavened bread. During the festival of Passover, matzah is eaten instead of bread.

Maya (Sanskrit). "Magic," a mystical and philosophical Hindu concept indicating that the world of common sensation is really a divine magical display that conceals the underlying reality of Brahman.

mehitzah (Hebrew). The "barrier" that separates the men's and women's sections of an Orthodox synagogue.

Massekhet Berakhot (Hebrew). Tractate on blessings, the first tractate of the Talmud.

Massekhet Niddah (Hebrew). Tractate on ritual impurity, the final tractate of the Talmud.

Midrash (Hebrew). Derived from *darash* ("interpret, explain, seek"). Stories, sermons, parables, and other non-halakhic materials explaining the Talmud. Also, the name of a text of these stories.

minyan (Hebrew). A prayer quorum of ten adult Jewish males.

Mi she-berakh (Hebrew). "May He Who blessed." A prayer for the welfare of a specific individual or group of individuals.

mitzvah (Hebrew, pl. *mitzvot*). Often translated as "commandment." There are said to be 613 *mitzvot* in the Torah. Of these, there are two types: *mishpatim* (sing. *mishpat*), rules governing relationships between humans, or civil law, which could be derived rationally; and *hukkim* (sing. *hok*), regulations governing the relationship between humans and God, ritual law, which are intrinsically mysterious.

moksha (Sanskrit). Spiritual liberation, freedom, the highest goal on Hinduism.

mondo (Japanese). The ritualized encounter between student and Zen master during a meditation retreat.

Mön-lam Chen-mo (Tibetan). "The Great Prayer Festival," instituted in Tibet by Tsong Khapa in the fifteenth century.

Motza'ei Shabbat (Hebrew). The evening after Shabbat, Saturday night.

mulla, mullali (Arabic and Persian). A "learned one," a Muslim religious leader.

murali (Sanskrit). The flute of Lord Krishna, also known as *bansuri* in Hindustani and *vamshi* in Sanskrit.

murti (Sanskrit). A statue or image of a Hindu or Buddhist deity.

na'ar (Hebrew). A male youth.

namaste (Hindi); **namaskar** (Sanskrit). "I salute you," a common, respectful form of greeting.

Ne'ilah (Hebrew). The "gate-closing" prayer at the conclusion of Yom Kippur.

neshamah (Hebrew). Soul.

nevu'ah (Hebrew). Prophecy.

nibbana (Pali). Enlightenment, spiritual liberation. In Sanskrit, *nirvana*. Cf. *moksha*.

nihum ha-avelim (Hebrew). "Comforting the bereaved." The *hiyuv* (obligation) to visit and bring solace to the bereaved.

nirvana (Sanskrit). See *nibbana*.

niggun (Hebrew; pl. *niggunim*) Wordless songs, melodies chanted as prayers, popularized in Hasidism.

Noahide commandments. According to rabbinic traditions, God gave seven commandments (*mitzvot*) to Noah and his descendants, which is to say to all humanity: not to murder, not to steal, not to bear false witness, not to be promiscuous, not to eat the limb of a living being, not to perform idolatry, and to establish a system of justice in the country. A righteous non-Jew who observes these seven commandments is called a *ben-Noah*, a child of Noah.

Nyingma (Tibetan). "The Ancient Ones," the oldest of the four sects of Tibetan Buddhism.

olam ha-ba (Hebrew). "The world to come."

Opshern (Yiddish). The customary first haircut given to a Jewish boy at age three, a festive event which also marks the beginning of his education.

or goyim (Hebrew). "A light to the nations," as taught by Prophet Isaiah (42:6, 49:6; cf. 60:3).

Ösel (Tibetan). "The clear light," the highest reality.

padayatra (Hindi, Sinhala). A march on foot, especially with political goals.

Pali. A Sanskritic language of North India in which the sacred texts of southern or Theravada Buddhism are written.

parokhet (Hebrew). The curtain that hangs before the *Aron ha-Kodesh* in synagogues. The original *parokhet* hung before the Holy of Holies in the Temple.

Passover. In Hebrew, Pesah; an eight-day spring festival that commemorates the Exodus from Egypt. It begins with a symbolic ritual meal known as the Seder, probably the most widely observed of all Judaic practices. The name refers to the Angel of Death's "passing over" the houses of the Israelites in Egypt.

phylacteries (Greek, English). See *tefillin*.

Pratimoksha (Sanskrit). The behavioral code for Buddhist monks and nuns.

peshat (Hebrew). The "plain" or literal meaning of a scared text, the first of the four levels of Biblical exegesis.

pukkha (Hindustani). Literally "ripe" or "cooked," the term means "substantial" or "proper."

Qur'an (Arabic). "The Recitation," the sacred text of Islam.

raga (Sanskrit). "That which enraptures," a classical melody.

rebbe (Yiddish). A spiritual teacher in Hasidic tradition.

rhobab (Persian). A stringed musical instrument, very popular in Afghanistan.

rickshawallah (Hindustani). One who pulls a rickshaw, a two-wheeled conveyance, through crowded streets. A menial and fast-disappearing occupation.

rinpoche (Tibetan). "Precious one," a suffixed title for a high lama.

rishi (Sanskrit). A seer, a mystic.

roshi (Japanese). Zen master.

sadhana (Sanskrit). A Buddhist or Hindu spiritual practice.

sadhu (Sanskrit). "Virtuous one," an itinerant Hindu holy man.

samskara (Sanskrit). A life-cycle ritual.

Sangha (Sanskrit). Community, the Buddhist order of monks and nuns.

sant (Hindi). A saint, derived from the Sanskrit *sat* ("true").

sardar, sardarji (Punjabi). A respectful term for a Sikh.

Sarvodaya Shramadana Movement. A Buddhist-inspired Sri Lankan non-governmental organization (NGO) dedicated to "the uplift of all," the meaning of *sarvodaya*.

sati (Pali). Mindfulness meditation.

satori (Japanese). A sudden, temporary experience of nirvana.

sekhel (Hebrew). Smartness, intelligence.

Seder (Hebrew). "Order," often used for the ritual meal (which follows a specified order) of Passover.

Sephardi (Hebrew). Jews whose ancestors came from Spain, or who follow their laws and customs.

Shabbat (Hebrew). The Biblical day of rest, which commences eighteen minutes before sundown on Friday and lasts until forty-two minutes (according to most opinions) after sundown on Saturday.

Shabbos (Yiddish). The Yiddish pronunciation of Shabbat.

Shaharit (Hebrew). Morning, or the morning prayer service.

shaikh, shuyukh (Arabic). "Leader," whether political, social, religious, or spiritual.

Shaiva (Sanskrit). Of or pertaining to Lord Shiva, a devotee of Shiva.

shammash (Hebrew). The caretaker of a synagogue.

Shambhala Buddhism. A contemporary school of western Buddhism created by Trungpa Rinpoche.

Shari'a (Arabic). "Highway," the system of Islamic law. Cf. *Halakhah.*

Shas (Hebrew). The Talmud. Acronym for *shishah sedarim* ("six orders"), the six major divisions that comprise the voluminous text.

Shekhinah (Hebrew). God's immanent aspect, often symbolized as female.

shelemut (Hebrew). Completeness, wholeness.

sheli'ah ha-am (Hebrew). My coinage, "emissary of the people."

shivah (Hebrew). "Seven," the seven days of intense morning that commences immediately after burial.

shivah minyan. It is customary for one who is "sitting *shivah*" to remain at home; a *shivah minyan* is the quorum of ten men who come to the mourner's home for the thrice-daily prayer services.

shloka (Sanskrit). A verse in epic meter, consisting of four lines of eight syllables each, or two lines of sixteen syllables each.

shofar (Hebrew). A ceremonial ram's or gazelle's horn, used on Rosh Hashanah (New Year) and Yom Kippur (Day of Atonement).

shtibl (Yiddish). A storefront synagogue.

shtrayml (Yiddish). A fur hat worn by some Hasidim to honor the Sabbath and festivals.

shul (Yiddish). "School," the term Orthodox Jews most frequently use for their synagogue.

shunyata (Sanskrit; in Tibetan *töngpanyi*). The highest reality according to Mahayana Buddhism, often translated as "emptiness" or "nothingness."
Sikh (Punjabi). From *shishya*, "student," a follower of the fifteenth-century Guru Nanak.

simhah (Hebrew). "Joy," any joyous occasion.

Singhalese, Sinhala. The people and the language of the majority ethnic group in Sri Lanka. The island is called "island of the Singhalese" in classical and medieval texts.

Siyum ha-Shas (Hebrew). A celebration upon "completion of the Talmud." In recent years it has become a huge, worldwide event culminating the seven-and-a-half year cycle of learning the Talmud known as *daf yomi* ("a page a day").

stupa (Sanskrit; in Tibetan *chorten*). A bell-shaped reliquary, ubiquitous in the Buddhist world, containing remains of the Buddha or a Buddhist saint.

Subud (Indonesian). A spiritual movement begun in Indonesia in the 1920s.

Sufi (Arabic). "One who wears a woolen cloak," a Muslim mystic.

Sukkot (Hebrew). Seven-day autumn festival during which observant Jews eat meals, relax, and perhaps sleep, in temporary huts of the same name, erected specifically for the festival and covered with wood or branches that allow starlight in. It is the only Jewish holiday called "the time of our joy," *zeman simhatenu.*

sutta, sutra (Pali, Sanskrit). Sacred texts in Buddhism.

swami (Sanskrit). "Lord," a respectful title for a Hindu monk, usually a *samnyasi*n, an initiated, orange-robed renunciate.

tallit (Hebrew). A prayer shawl.

Talmud (Aramaic). "Teaching," the Oral Torah, written in Aramaic, a record of rabbinic discussions pertaining to Jewish law, ethics, customs, and history.

It consists of six "orders" (*sedarim*), and therefore is alternatively known as the *Shas* (*shishah*, or six, *sedarim*), and sixty-three tractates, or *massekhtot*. There are two versions of the Talmud, the better-known, having been composed in Babylon, known as the *Bavli*, and the other in Israel, known as the *Yerushalmi*.

Tanakh (Hebrew). Traditional acronym designating the Hebrew Bible, built from the initial letters of its three divisions: *Torah* (the Five Books of Moses), *Nevi'im* (the prophetic and historical works), and *Ketuvim* (the writings, such as Esther, Lamentations, Song of Songs, Psalms, etc.).

Tantra, Tantric (Sanskrit). A class of Hindu, Jain, and Buddhist texts, as well as a religious style that has been widespread in India since early medieval times. *Tantric* has become synonymous with esoteric in that it employs magical and ecstatic techniques and metaphors. One who practices *Tantra* is called a *Tantrika*. *Tantrayana* is the path of Tantra.

Tanya (Aramaic). The core text of Habad Hasidism, written by Rabbi Shneur Zalman in the eighteenth century.

tawa, lam, draybu (Tibetan). "View, path, and goal," a Tibetan method for analyzing philosophical or religious beliefs and practices.

tefillin (Hebrew). Two black leather boxes containing scrolls of parchment inscribed with Biblical verses. The arm-*tefillin*, or *shel yad*, is worn on the upper arm, while the head-*tefillin*, or *shel rosh*, is placed above the forehead. According to Jewish law, they should be worn during weekday morning prayer services. Sometimes known in English as *phylacteries*, from the Greek.

teshuvah (Hebrew). "Return." (1) A written response to a question (*she'elah, shaila*) about Jewish law or practice. (2) To return to God, hence "repentance."

thangka (Tibetan). A sacred scroll painting, usually of a deity or *mandala* (mystical diagram).

Theravada (Pali). "The Way of the Elders," the dominant form of Buddhism in south and southeast Asia.

tikkun (Hebrew). "To repair" or "mend." In Jewish mysticism, a *tikkun* is the set of lessons one must learn in a particular *gilgul* or reincarnation; thus it is one's "life task." In contemporary socially active Judaism, *tikkun* means to repair the world.

Tishah be-Av (Hebrew). The ninth day of the month of Av, a solemn fast-day to commemorate the great Jewish national tragedies, including the destruction of both the First and Second Temples, and the expulsion from Spain in 1492.

töngpanyi (Tibetan, in Sanskrit *shunyata*). The highest reality according to Mahayana Buddhism, often translated as "emptiness" or "nothingness."

Triple Gem, Triple Refuge. The Buddha, the Dharma, and the Sangha.

tzaddik (Hebrew). A fully righteous person, a saint.

tulku (Tibetan). A "reincarnating lama."

Upanishads (Sanskrit). Mystical Hindu texts believed to have been written between around 900 and 600 B.C.E.

Vajrayana (Sanskrit). "The Adamantine Vehicle," synonymous with Tantric Buddhism.

Veda (Sanskrit). "Knowledge," the most central sacred texts of Hinduism, said to date from the middle of the second millennium B.C.E.

Vedanta (Sanskrit). Literally, "the culmination of the Vedas," the term as used today refers to the non-dualist system of thought promulgated by the eighth-century Hindu philosopher Shamkara.

vipassana (Pali). A Buddhist meditation technique for the cultivation of insight.

yana (Sanskrit). "Career" or "vehicle," a way of talking about different forms of Buddhism.

yehidut (Hebrew). A period of seclusion of the newly married couple when they break the fast of the wedding day and, in times past, consummated the marriage. In Hasidism, the intimate one-on-one form of spiritual teaching between a rebbe and his student.

yeshiva (Hebrew). An institution of religious education.

Yiddish. A vernacular of medieval German mixed with words from Hebrew, Polish, Russian, and other languages. First-generation American Jews called their dialect "Yinglish."

yoga (Sanskrit). Cognate of the English "yoke"; its literal meaning is to harness or to place under discipline; therefore, a spiritual discipline.

Yortsayt (Yiddish, from German *Jahrzeit*). The annual memorial of a deceased person.

zafu (Japanese). A meditation cushion.

zazen (Japanese). Zen meditation.

Zen (Japanese). A Japanese form of Buddhism emphasizing meditation; the word *zen* derives from the Pali *jhana*, then the Sanskrit *dhyana*, which in Chinese became *ch'an* and in Korean *son*.

zendo (Japanese). A Zen meditation hall.

Who's Who in This Book

~

Ariyararatne, A. T. (1931–). Dubbed Sri Lanka's "Little Gandhi," Ari is the founder of the Sarvodaya Shramadana Movement, the largest NGO is the country. Based on the Mahatma's philosophy as applied in his Buddhist country, Sarvodaya works for village uplift, basic needs, ethnic understanding, education, and women's rights.

Aurobindo Ghose, Sri (1872–1950). Utopian and evolutionary, Sri Aurobindo was one of the architects of modern Hinduism. He called his teachings "Integral Yoga," and founded an intentional community called Auroville near Pondicherry in South India.

Berzin, Alexander (1944–). A native of Paterson, New Jersey, Berzin earned a Ph.D. at Harvard in 1972. He lived in Dharamsala, India, from 1969 to 1988, was a founding member of the Translations Bureau of the Library of Tibetan Works and Archives, and served as secretary and interpreter for the Dalai Lama. He is a respected Buddhist teacher whose work is available on-line at BerzinArchives.com. He lives in Berlin, Germany.

Bhajan, Yogi (1929–2004). Born Haribhajan Singh, he was a Sikh teacher and the founder of the "Happy, Healthy, Holy Organization." He taught kundalini yoga and promoted vegetarianism. He became a U.S. citizen, and was known for providing free food at rock concerts and be-ins during the 1960s.

Bhaktivedanta, Swami A. C. Prabhupada (1896–1977). The founder of the International Society for Krishna Consciousness (ISKCON, or the "Hare Krishna" movement), whose disciples are known in America for their practice of *kirtan*, the ecstatic and public chanting of the name of Krishna.

Blofeld, John (1913–1987). Educated at Cambridge, he spent most of his life in China and Thailand. Fluent in Chinese and a tantric adept, he translated the *I Ching* from the Chinese and wrote numerous books, including *The Tantric Mysticism of Tibet*.

Brown, Judith Simmer (1946–). Professor of religious studies at Naropa University and a senior teacher of Shambhala Buddhist meditation, Judith is the author of *Dakini's Warm Breath*.

Brown, Richard C. (1948–). Professor and chair of Naropa University's unique department of contemplative education, Richard is certified as a teacher of Vajradhatu Buddhist meditation.

Campbell, Hugh H. (1905–1981). Landscape artist who lived as a recluse in the woods of Mount Holly, New Jersey, and became a disciple of Swami Yatiswarananda of the Ramakrishna Order in 1942. Author of *Knock Vigorously to Be Heard*.

Carlebach, Shlomo (1925–1994). Born in Germany, Carlebach received rabbinic ordination from the sixth Lubavitcher Rebbe. He and Rabbi Zalman M. Schachter-Shalomi (*see below*) were the first emissaries of the Rebbe to American colleges in the 1950s. Charismatic and effusive, Reb Shlomo became an icon of the *baal-teshuvah* movement of "returnees" to traditional Judaism. Known as the "singing rabbi," Carlebach and his guitar became familiar sights in San Francisco's Haight-Ashbury, where he founded the House of Love and Prayer in 1967. His liturgical melodies are extremely popular in the Jewish world, where a "Carlebach minyan" is synonymous with tuneful and ecstatic prayer.

Chefitz, Mitchell (1941–). A line officer in the U.S. Navy who served in Vietnam, Mitch was founding rabbi of the Havurah of South Florida, an innovative "synagogue without walls," for twenty-two years. As senior rabbi of Temple Israel of Greater Miami, he guided the renewal of the once-prominent downtown Reform synagogue, where he is now scholar-in-residence. He has written several novels, including *The Seventh Telling: The Kabbalah of Moshe Katan* and *Curse of Blessings*, as well as books of poetry and short stories, and is a respected teacher of Kabbalah.

Chidanand Saraswati, Swami (1952–). Also known as Pujya Swami, he is a very popular and influential Hindu teacher, the founder of Parmarth Niketan in Rishikesh, India.

Chödron, Venerable Thubten (1950–). Raised in a Jewish home in California, and ordained in the Gelukpa Order in 1977, she is highly respected as a

meditation teacher. She founded Sravasti Abbey, a Buddhist monastery and re-
treat center not far from Spokane, Washington. She is the author of *Blossoms of Dharma: Life as a Buddhist Nun* and has written about her Jewish background.

Chubb, Jehangir N. (1910–). Disciple of Sri Aurobindo Ghose, Chubb is a philosopher who taught for a time at Temple University. His best-known book is *Assertion and Fact: The Categories of Self-Conscious Thinking.*

Clark, Robert A. (1908–2001). A Jungian psychiatrist, Clark studied medi-
cine at Pittsburgh and psychiatry in Switzerland, and then became chief of psychiatry at Friends Hospital in Philadelphia. He wrote *Six Lectures on Jung's Psychology* and *The Quaker Heritage in Medicine.*

Dalai Lama, His Holiness, the Fourteenth (Venerable Tenzin Gyatsho) (1935–). One of the world's most beloved personalities, the Dalai Lama is the supreme leader of the Gelukpa Order of Tibetan Buddhism, head of the Government-in-Exile of Tibet, Nobel Peace laureate (1989), and recipient of the U.S. Congressional Gold Medal (2007).

Dharmasiri, Gunapala (1942–). Once a Theravada Buddhist monk and now a retired professor of philosophy at Peradeniya University, Sri Lanka, Dharmé wrote *A Buddhist Critique of the Christian Concept of God* and *Fundamentals of Buddhist Ethics.*

Dodrup Chen Rinpoche (1927–). The fourth in his *tulku* lineage, he is one of the most highly respected teachers of the Nyingma ("Ancient Ones") Order of Tibetan Buddhism. He is known for transmitting the Dzogchen ("Great Perfection") teachings, considered among the highest esoteric systems in Buddhism. He lives in Gangtok, Sikkim.

Einhorn, Ira (1940–). A leader of the counterculture in Philadelphia during the 1960s, Einhorn is a self-styled philosopher who was convicted of mur-
dering and dismembering his girlfriend and hiding her body in a steamer trunk in his closet. He fled to Europe and fought extradition. He is currently serving a life term in Houtzdale Prison in Pennsylvania.

Faruqi, Isma'il R. (1921–1986). A Palestinian imam and jurist, Faruqi taught at Syracuse, McGill, and Temple. In 1986, he and his wife were murdered in their home in the Philadelphia suburbs.

Friedman, Maurice S. (1921–). A professor at Sarah Lawrence College, the New School for Social Research, Temple University, and San Diego State University, Friedman is best known for applying Martin Buber's dialogical philosophy to psychotherapy, the study of religions, and comparative literature. He is co-director of the Institute for Dialogical Psychotherapy and won the National Jewish Book Award in 1985 for *Martin Buber: The Life of Dialogue*.

Ginsberg, Allen (1926–1997). Beat poet and peace activist, he was founder and head of the Jack Kerouac School of Disembodied Poetics at Naropa University. His best-known work is *Howl*, a poetic manifesto of the Beat movement.

Gordis, Robert (1908–1992). Conservative rabbi and mainstay at the Jewish Theological Seminary in New York, he taught for a time at Temple. He translated several books of the Bible into English, and is the author of *The Book of God and Man: A Study of Job* and *Love and Sex: A Modern Jewish Perspective*.

Greenberg, Blu (1936–). Writer, lecturer, and founder of the Jewish Orthodox Feminist Alliance (JOFA) in New York City, she wrote *How to Run a Traditional Jewish Household, On Women and Judaism: A View from Tradition*, and *Black Bread: Poems After the Holocaust*. She has an M.A. in clinical psychology from CUNY and an M.S. in Jewish history from Yeshiva University. She is married to Rabbi Irving Greenberg.

Greenberg, Irving "Yitz" (1933–). Author, scholar, and community leader, he earned his Ph.D. in history at Harvard and served as rabbi of the Riverdale (N.Y.) Jewish Center while teaching at Yeshiva University. He founded the Center for Learning and Leadership (CLAL) and wrote *Jewish Teachings to Perfect the World*. He is married to Blu Greenberg.

Kamenetz, Rodger (1950–). Professor of English and Religious Studies at Louisiana State University, he wrote *The Jew in the Lotus* about the Dharamsala dialogue between eight Jewish scholars and rabbis, and the Dalai Lama. He also wrote *Stalking Elijah*, for which he won the National Jewish Book Award, *About Last Night's Dream*, and several volumes of poetry.

Kapleau Roshi, Philip (1912–2004). A Jewish-born Zen master, Kapleau was chief Allied court reporter at the Nuremberg Trials, and he later led meditation-witness pilgrimages to Auschwitz. He founded the Rochester

Zen Center. He wrote many books; the most highly regarded is *The Three Pillars of Zen*.

Karmapa, The Sixteenth Gwalya (1924–1981). The supreme head of the Kagyupa Order of Tibetan Buddhism, the Karmapa Lama was best known for the "Black Crown Ceremony," a mystic rite he conducted while wearing a hat said to be woven from *dakini* hair. After fleeing Tibet, he established his monastic seat at Rumtek, near Gangtok, Sikkim.

Khan, Pir Vilayat (1916–2004). Born in London, he succeeded his father as *murshid* (spiritual leader) of the Chisti Order of Sufism. Khan taught extensively in Europe and America. The Chisti Order, founded in the tenth century in Afghanistan, is focused on Ajmer, India, where Moinuddin Chisti popularized it during the thirteenth century. It is known for its openness to non-Muslims, as well as its meditative practices.

Khema, Ayyah (1923–1997). Born in a Jewish family in Berlin, she was raised in Shanghai and became interested in spirituality. After raising a family in California, she became a Buddhist nun, established a meditation center in Sri Lanka, and became a leader in the Buddhist women's movement. She taught meditation around the globe, but spent much of the latter part of her life in her native Germany.

Leary, Timothy (1920–1996). As the *Wikipedia* succinctly recounts his life, he "was an American writer, psychologist, modern pioneer and advocate of psychedelic drug research and use, and one of the first people whose remains have been sent into space. An icon of 1960s counterculture, Leary is most famous as a proponent of the therapeutic and spiritual benefits of LSD. He coined and popularized the catch phrase 'Turn on, tune in, drop out.' "

Levitt, Joy (1954–). Reconstructionist rabbi and executive director of the Jewish Community Center in Manhattan, she is author *of A Night of Questions: A Passover Haggadah*.

Lipskar, Sholom Dovber (1946–). Born in Tashkent, Russia, Lipskar was a leading student of the Seventh Lubavitcher Rebbe. He founded the Landow Yeshiva in Miami Beach in 1969, the Shul of Bay Harbor in Surfside in 1981, the Aleph Institute, which provides pastoral and counseling services to Jews in the military and in prisons, in 1981, and the Chaim Yakov Shlomo College of Jewish Studies in 2004.

Ma Jayasati Bhagavati (1940–). Guru, AIDS activist, artist, and poet, Ma is the popular, controversial leader of the Kashi Ashram, which she founded in 1976 in Sebastian, Florida. She was born into a poor Jewish family in Brooklyn as Joyce Green. Her teaching is essentially devotional and tries to encompass all faiths. She is a disciple of Neem Karoli Baba, who was also guru to Baba Ram Dass.

Maharishi Mahesh Yogi (1917–2008). The founder of Transcendental Meditation and best known as the "guru to the stars," including the Beatles and Mia Farrow, Maharishi announced his retirement to his home in Holland, went into silence, and passed away early in 2008.

Mahathera, Venerable Nyanaponika (1901–1994). Born a German Jew named Siegmund Feninger, he became a Buddhist monk in 1936 in Sri Lanka, where he co-founded the Buddhist Publication Society in 1958. He lived much of his life in his Forest Hermitage near Kandy and wrote *Abhidhamma Studies: Buddhist Explorations in Consciousness and Time* and *The Vision of Dhamma*.

Malekar, Ezekiel Isaac (1945–). Deputy registrar (law) in the National Human Rights Commission, New Delhi, and head of the Jewish community in New Delhi.

Mendes-Flohr, Paul (1941–). Professor of modern Jewish thought at the Divinity School of the University of Chicago and at the Hebrew University, he is a leading scholar of both Franz Rosenzweig and Martin Buber. He is the author of *Post-Traditional Jewish Identities* and a number of other works.

Muktananda, Swami (1908–1982). Founder of the Siddha Yoga movement in America, he was best known for *shaktipat*, a practice said to stimulate mystical experience by touch. His teaching was based on the tradition of Kashmir Shaivism and involved the practice of *kundalini* yoga. His best-known book is *The Play of Consciousness*.

Murti, T. R. V. (1902–1986). Generally regarded as one of India's leading twentieth-century philosophers, Murti was a professor and head of the philosophy department at Benares Hindu University. Trained in both traditional and modern philosophic traditions, he had a photographic memory and a passion for respectful disputations. His *Central Philosophy of Buddhism* is considered a masterpiece.

Nikhilananda, Swami (1895–1973). A monk of the Ramakrishna Order of non-dualistic Hinduism, he founded the New York Ramakrishna-Vivekananda Center in 1933. He translated several important Hindu texts into English, including the *Upanishads*, the *Bhagavad Gita*, and Shankara's *Atma-Bodha*, and he wrote *The Gospel of Sri Ramakrishna*.

Omer-Man, Jonathan (1934–). A California-based Kabbalist, he is the founder of Mitivta: A Center for Contemplative Judaism. He is retired and lives in Berkeley.

Phillips, Bernard (1917–1974). The founding chair of the department of religion at Temple University, he was one of the architects of the American Academy of Religion in 1963. He was a student of Yasutoni Roshi, a well-known Zen master. Phillips wrote an influential essay on "Zen and Humanism" and was editor of D. T. Suzuki's classic, *The Essentials of Zen Buddhism*.

Palmo, K. T. Khechog (1911–1977). The first western woman ever to become a Tibetan Buddhist nun, she received ordination at the age of fifty-five from her teacher, the Sixteenth Karmapa Lama. Before ordination, her name was Frieda Bedi, and she was the wife of a Sikh spiritual teacher, Baba Bedi, and mother of Bollywood star Kabir. She became involved with the resettlement of Tibetan refugees in 1959. She taught worldwide, translated many Tibetan texts, especially prayers to the savioress Tara, and was the subject of a biography by Sheila Fugard, *Lady of Realisation: Tribute to Sister Palmo*.

Rabbani, Mulla Burhanuddin (1940–). A Tadjik from northern Afghanistan, he graduated from Egypt's al-Azhar University and became head of the Faculty of Islamic Law at Kabul University. He narrowly escaped arrest by the Soviet occupiers of his country and became a political leader of the Northern Alliance of *mujahiddin*. Rabbani's forces were the first to return to Kabul after the Soviets were expelled, and he served as president of Afghanistan between

1992 and 1996. When the Taliban seized power, he was again forced to flee for his life.

Rahula, Walpola (1907–1997). Highly respected Sri Lankan Buddhist monk, he was vice-chancellor of Vidyalankara University in Sri Lanka and the first monk to hold a professorship at a western university (Northwestern University in 1964). His *What the Buddha Taught* is one of the very best introductions to Buddhism, and his *History of Buddhism in Ceylon* is a standard work on the subject.

Ram Dass, Baba (Richard Alpert) (1931–). Born into a wealthy and prominent Jewish family in Newton, Massachusetts, he was dismissed from Harvard's faculty for LSD experiments, along with his colleague Timothy Leary (*see above*). He traveled to India and became a disciple of Neem Karoli Baba, was given the name Baba Ram Dass, and founded a spiritual center in Taos, New Mexico. His *Be Here Now* was an unofficial bible of the hippie counterculture.

Ray, Reginald A. (1943–). The first Buddhist Studies faculty member at Naropa University and *acharya* (senior teacher) of Shambhala Buddhism, he is one of Chogyam Trungpa Rinpoche's first American students. He is the author of *Buddhist Saints in India* and *Indestructible Truth,* and runs a retreat center in Crestone, Colorado.

Riff, Naphtali Zvi Yehudah (1894–1976). The longtime rabbi of Congregation Sons of Israel in Camden, New Jersey, he made *aliyah* to Israel in 1966 and settled in Bnei Brak. He was president of Ezrat Torah, a charitable institution in Jerusalem.

Schachter-Shalomi, Zalman Meshullam (1924–). Born in Poland and raised in Vienna, he survived the Holocaust and came to the United States, where he received ordination at the Central Lubavitch Yeshiva. The Sixth Rebbe sent him and Rabbi Shlomo Carlebach (*see above*) to be emissaries to college students. He studied psychology and religion at Boston University, and taught at the University of Manitoba, Temple University, and Naropa University, where he held the World Wisdom Chair. Along the way, he broke with Orthodoxy and is considered the *zeyde* (grandfather) of the Jewish Renewal Movement. Reb Zalman is author of *Jewish with Feeling* and *From Age-ing to Sage-ing.*

Schneerson, Menachem Mendel (the Lubavitcher Rebbe) (1902–1994). The Seventh (and last) Lubavitcher Rebbe, he was without doubt one of the most influential figures in twentieth-century Judaism and in American religion in general. Born in the Ukraine, he received ordination in 1923 and then studied sciences in Berlin and Paris until the Nazi occupation. He settled in Crown Heights in Brooklyn in 1941, and succeeded his father-in-law, Yosef Yitzhok Schneersohn, as leader of the Habad movement of Hasidic Judaism. Charismatic, visionary, and according to some a miracle worker and even the Messiah, he transformed a small and reclusive Hasidic sect into a highly visible movement with schools and synagogues seemingly everywhere. He published voluminously in Hebrew and Yiddish, including *Likkutei Sihot*, thirty-nine volumes of his discourses, a Passover Haggadah, and *Ha-Yom Yom*, a collection of mystical aphorisms arranged by the calendar. He was posthumously awarded the U.S. Congressional Gold Medal; at the award ceremony President Clinton hailed his "outstanding and enduring contributions toward world education, morality, and acts of charity."

Seo, Venerable Kung-bo (1914–1996). A Zen master of the Korean Chogye Order and a calligraphy master, he was the author of *A Study of Korean Zen Buddhism*.

Sharma, L. N. (1931–). Successor to his mentor, Professor T. R. V. Murti (*see above*), as head of the department of philosophy at Benares Hindu University, he is the author of *Kashmir Saivism*. He lives in retirement in Jaipur.

Shifman, Mordechai (1966–). Principal of Judaic Studies at Hebrew Academy, Miami Beach, and a highly respected Talmud teacher, he is regarded as the foremost disciple of Rabbi Yohanan Zweig, head of Talmudic University in Miami Beach.

Singh, Sant Kirpal (1894–1974). He was a Sikh teacher of *surat shabd yoga*, which he taught as "the underlying thread of the esoteric Sound Current (Shabd, Naam, or Word) as the root experience of the Saints." He was associated with the esoteric Radha Soami Satsang and founded the "Unity of Man" movement, teaching that the universal brotherhood of man could be realized only on the basis of the universal fatherhood of God.

Steinsaltz, Adin (1937–). One of the most respected rabbis in the world, he is the author of more than sixty books, including his translation of the Talmud, an esoteric interpretation of Kabbalah entitled *The Thirteen-Petalled Rose*, and a translation and commentary on the *Tanya*, the seminal work of Habad Hasidism. He is *nasi* (president) of the reconstituted Jerusalem Sanhedrin, the highest Jewish court.

Stolper, Akiva (1956–). Rabbi of Congregation Ohr Chaim in Miami Beach from 1995 to 2008.

Sivananda, Swami (1887–1973). Highly respected teacher of yoga and non-dualism, he founded the Divine Life Society in Rishikesh. Among his 296 (!) books, the best-known is *Yoga of Synthesis*.

Tenzin, Geshe Lobsang (1927–). Born Satya Dev Negi in Kinnaur, a Tibetan-speaking region in the Indian Himalayas, Geshe-la was ordained a Buddhist monk by the Dalai Lama at the age of fourteen. He earned the *geshe lharampa* degree, the highest in traditional Tibetan education, at Drepung Loseling Monastery in South India in 1994, and a Ph.D. at Emory University in Atlanta in 1999. He is senior lecturer in the department of religion at Emory and founder of the Drepung Loseling Institute in Atlanta.

Trungpa Rinpoche, Chögyam (1939–1987). One of the major figures responsible for disseminating Tibetan Buddhism in the west, as well as one of the most controversial, he characterized his teachings as "crazy wisdom." A master of the Kagyupa Order, he founded Naropa University in 1974 to foster creative interactions between east and west. Spontaneous poetics, contemplative education, and contemplative psychology are among the unique Naropa programs he inspired. He envisioned and established Shambhala Buddhism, which focuses on appreciation of the sacredness of everyday life. Among his many books are *Cutting Through Spiritual Materialism* and *Shambhala: The Sacred Path of the Warrior*.

Vivekananda, Swami (1863–1902). One of the most influential leaders of the "Hindu renaissance," as well as an ardent nationalist, he was a disciple of the celebrated Kali devotee Ramakrishna Paramahamsa, and founder of the Ramakrishna Math and Mission. He is best known in the west for his oration at the 1893 World Parliament of Religions in Chicago, and for founding several Vedanta Society branches. He is a hero in contemporary Indian culture.

Waldoks, Moshe (1949–). Rabbi of Temple Beth Zion in Brookline, Massachusetts, he is author of *The Big Book of Jewish Humor*.

Wiesel, Elie (1928–). Novelist, Holocaust survivor, mystic, and 1986 Nobel Peace Prize laureate, he is a professor at Boston University and an internationally revered voice of conscience. Among his forty books, his Holocaust memoir, *Night*, is best known; his book *Souls on Fire* is a moving description of Hasidism. He received the U.S. Congressional Gold Medal in 1985, as well as numerous other honors.

Yadav, Bibhuti S. (1943–1999). Among the most outstanding students of T. R. V. Murti (*see above*) at Benares Hindu University, he spent his academic career at Temple University. Humorous, challenging, and eccentric, his unique teaching style was unfailingly appreciated by his students (including me). He wrote a number of important articles about Madhyamaka Buddhism.

Yeshe, Lama Thubten (1935–1984). A teacher in the Gelukpa Order, he founded Kopan Monastery in Nepal and the Foundation for the Preservation of Mahayana Heritage. His best-known book is *Wisdom Energy*, and he also wrote *Becoming Your Own Therapist*.

Zalman, Shneur (the Alter Rebbe) (1745–1812). Author of *Tanya*, he was the architect of Habad Hasidism. Didactic and mystical, his writings continue to challenge and stimulate serious readers. He is known as the Alter Rebbe, the first teacher of Habad, and a second-generation disciple of the Baal Shem Tov, the founder of Hasidism.